THE PRIME OF LIFE

Edited by

Liz Wakefield

First published in Great Britain in 2002 by
POETRY NOW
Remus House,
Coltsfoot Drive,
Peterborough, PE2 9JX
Telephone (01733) 898101
Fax (01733) 313524

HB ISBN 0 75432 810 4
SB ISBN 0 75432 811 2

FOREWORD

Although we are a nation of poets we are accused of not reading poetry, or buying poetry books. After many years of listening to the incessant gripes of poetry publishers, I can only assume that the books they publish, in general, are books that most people do not want to read.

Poetry should not be obscure, introverted, and as cryptic as a crossword puzzle: it is the poet's duty to reach out and embrace the world.

The world owes the poet nothing and we should not be expected to dig and delve into a rambling discourse searching for some inner meaning.

The reason we write poetry (and almost all of us do) is because we want to communicate: an ideal; an idea; or a specific feeling. Poetry is as essential in communication, as a letter; a radio; a telephone, and the main criterion for selecting the poems in this anthology is very simple: they communicate.

My Freshly Made Bed.

On page 42.

Written by:-

Susan Carole Roberts

CONTENTS

Summer In The Garden	Edwin Page	1
My Home	E Joan Knight	2
Dancing In Limbo	Caroline Rachael Gandy	3
T	Charles David Jenkins	4
Mire Fire!	John L Wright	5
This Bad Hair Day	Judith Thomas	6
Animal Instincts	Paul Foreman	7
A Hard Fact	Muriel Willa	8
I'm Getting Old!	Angela Jones	9
Ben	Rebekah Jones	10
More Than Money Can Buy	Suzy Talbot	11
My Square World	Kopan Mahadeva	12
Light In His Darkness	P J Littlefield	13
Surfing The Web	Audrey Allott	14
Free Paper Brightlingsea Chronicle	Norma Langley	15
Nikki	D Townshend	16
To Gilbert	Vivienne Brocklehurst	17
Little Tom	Pauline Nind	18
The Best Things In Life	Margaret Marklew	19
I Like Cats	Margaret Whitton	20
My Heart Burns For The Pennines	Heys Stuart Wolfenden	21
Cornwall	Ann Hathaway	22
Best Things In Life	Edith Antrobus	23
A Natural Gift	Helen-Elaine Oliver	24
Small Things	D Bruce	25
Lotte's Cooking	John Crowe	26
Silence Of The Birds	Norman Meadows	28
Trainers	Barbara J Kerks	29
My Favourite Place	Marilyn Wellman	30
For My Precious Pussy Cat	Marcella Pellow	31
The Hunting Mime	Katie Johnson	32
Mommy	Christopher Higgins	33
Some Things That Are Free	J Vessey	34
Why Trees?	D P R	35
Willett The Philosopher	Clive Cornwall	36

The Gospel Ship	Frances Gibson	37
She Is Simply The Best	Clare Allen	38
Honey Bun	Mary Skelton	39
A Little Gentleman In My Life	Parveen K Saini	40
Cuckmere's Moment	Lorna Tippett	41
My Freshly Made Bed	Susan Carole Roberts	42
Glory Of The Hills	Derek Pile	43
Best Things In Life	Pauline Drew	44
French Windows And Railings	D Sawyer	45
Blessed Is The Life You Live	Jim Cuthbert	46
For Our Love Of Trevor!	Graham Mitchell & Amy Kelly	47
At The Hairdressers	Betty Hattersley	48
A Poetic 'Genius'		
Sees The Funny Side	Brigid Smith	49
I Remember	R Bissett	50
Dog Train Afternoon	Jane Phillimore	51
Childhood Trips	Julie Powell	52
All We Like Hebrides	John Crowe	53
The Sun	Maureen Thomas	54
Two Pretty Pussy Cats	Helen Barwood	55
A Sinking Feeling	Nicky Chaperlin	56
Coming And Going	Evelyn Balmain	57
A PG Tip	Martin Winbolt-Lewis	58
Strange Happenings	Terry Burrows	59
Smiles And Laughter	Robert Waggitt	60
Diva At The Village Dance	Jill I Henderson	61
Probeverbs	Ato Ulzen-Appiah	62
Ducks Of Cuerden Park	Robert Allen	63
A Pawn In The Game	Stuart Delvin	64
Getting Dressed	Catherine Champion	65
Best Night Out	J Gatenby	66
Good Advice	Jean Saunders	67
Hotel Pool	Wendy Kirkpatrick	68
Out Of The Mouths . . .	Susan Wilson	69
Kiss	Les Merton	70
It Comes To Us All	Beryl R Daintree	71
I Am A Poet - But I		
Didn't Know It	Derek Harvey	72

Noses	E M Budge	74
Frozen Stiff	Gillian Mullett	75
The Fly	Dennis Young	76
A Fool's Paradise	T A Eady	77
It's Fun	Janet Cavill	78
Our Vicar	David Varley	79
Colourful Characters	Catherine Craft	80
Phenomenon Fatigue	Corinne Lovell	81
A Chocolate Cake	Patricia A Taylor	82
One Man And His Dog	Hilary Jill Robson	83
'Sexty' Years Young!	Doreen M Carne	84
The Thrill Of The Twilight Years	Anthony J Gibson	85
Creative Writing Class 1-4-2000	Richard Birch	86
Those People	Hugh Campbell	87
Bees With Fleas!	Kerri Fordham	88
Anything But That!	Fred Grimwade	89
Blind Date	Sarah Blackmore	90
Gray And Debbo On Honeymoon	H G Griffiths	91
A Weedy Limerick	Roma Davies	92
A Limerick	P Allen	93
Our Mavis And Her Fella	G Livermore	94
Little Hyena	Martin Snowdon	95
January Sales	Ken Price	96
Venus De Milo	Alan Pow	97
Breezy Brummie	Geoffrey Woodhead	98
Donor Problems	Derek B Hewertson	99
Happiness	D Adams	100
Jim	B Eyre	101
Don't Pick Your Nose	Lynda J Smith	102
Saint	Kristina Howells	103
Phobic Aerobic	Maureen Reynolds	104
Gift	Michael Fenton	105
Maestro	F Baker	106
Pure Laughter	Christine Nicholls	107
My Silver Reindeer	A E Doney	108
Waking Up	Jackie Stapleton	110
Family	Noor Shahzadi	111
Lament For The Trolley-Bus	Geoffrey Matthews	112

Gardens	Kathy Prince	114
Best Things	Ann Bryce	115
The Vision Of Heaven	I Lindo	116
Flora	Violet M Corlett	117
A Beach In Winter	Dora Watkins	118
Look Out	Roland Seager	119
Let Me Have My Life Back Please	M D Bedford	120
Ode To A Tigress	V Barrasin	121
One Man's Inspiration	Lyn Sandford	122
Little Things	T M Webster	123
My Favourite Sight	Val Spall	124
The Pearl Of Flowers	Margaret M Donnelly	125
My Wedding Gown	Linda Cooper	126
Is This Art?	Janet Fludder	127
Alive	Barry Welburn	128
Joy	Helen Persse	129
Nine To Five	Barbara R Lockwood	130
Best Things In Life	Beryl Moorehead	131
The Day You Left Me	Pamela M Wild	132
Paragons Of Pleasure	Tree	133
The Sgwd Yr Elra Waterfall Walk	Christine Licence	134
The Beach At Southwold	Carmel Wright	135
Pride Of Place	M Hanmer	136
The Great Outdoors	Sheila Walters	137
Best Things In Life	Joyce Peter	138
Me And You And A Dog Named Boo	Rachael Poyle	139
Summer In Portugal	Colin Skilton	140
My Pets	Irene Millington	141
Hillside Thoughts	Arthur Pickles	142
I Believe In Love	Flora Passant	143
The Swallows Of Portugal	Margaret Findlay	144
Dragon On An Orange Wall	Stewart Gordon	145
Journeying	Michael Soper	146
Lady	Ann Simpson	147
My Furry Friend	Evelyn M Harding	148
My Favourite Things	Jean P Edwards McGovern	149

Our Mum	Helen Posgate	150
Willow	J W Murison	151
The Ball	Jillian Shields	152
Children's Innocence	Lesley J Worrall	153
The Unicorn	Pamela Dickson	154
You Make Us So Proud . . .	Ron Matthews Jr	155
Snoopy My Cat	Margaret Kelly	156
Meditation On The Sun	C Warren-Gash	157
The Lane	John Wiltshire	158
Warming Days	A May	159
Free Time	M A Challis	160
Bridges	Leslie Fine	161
Best Things In Life Are Free	E M Crellin	162
Guess Who?	Norma Macarthur	163
The Cardboard Kisses	Channon Cornwallis	164
A Cuppa	Michael Widdop	165

SUMMER IN THE GARDEN

The buddleia is alive with life;
Probing, flitting, buzzing, searching,
Bees and butterflies in cohabitation
Through hours of warm sunlight,
Busy in life-affirming activity,
Ignorant of their beauty,
Which I perceive,
Sitting on a nearby bench,
Spellbound by the colours and movements,
Smiling at this interplay of existence,
Knowing that Eden is right here.

Edwin Page

My Home

Like a warm, comforting garment
You encircled us; we felt safe
Within amongst favourite things:
Familiar furniture, books,
Music, equipment for our skills.
Then, through altered circumstances,
Life took on another meaning.
First, I considered leaving you
But memories and ties were strong
And your outlook greatly treasured.
I retained the tried and trusted,
Continue to use my assets.

Outside, my garden, a record
Of past and present hopes, brings back
Recollections of two people
At nurseries, shared decisions
On plant requirements, layout plans,
Physical work allocations.
Now, one individual's toil
Endeavours to retain a landscape
Pleasing to the eyes and a refuge
For birds and little wild creatures.

From the main front bedroom window,
Distance provides views of places
Once frequented with another.
Season varied fields and small woods
Remind me of a former life.
Today, these scenes offer suggestions
For writing and other types of
Artistic creativity.

E Joan Knight

DANCING IN LIMBO

A sea horse
scarred on my skin
A memory
tattooed on my heart
Of a happiness
complete

Sea sprays
and sun's rays
In a yester life
of cloudless days
My last link
to life
before
Death

Lost in a lavender field
A sweet aroma
comforted the clouds
into remission
Strangling troubles
with a golden chain

The sun baked
a fictionary
of health
As waves lapped
at sanguine feet
dancing in limbo.

Caroline Rachael Gandy

T

T is for two.
T is for me.
T is for golfers.
T is for tea.
T is for pot.
T is for tops.
T is for shirt,
Upon which the tea slops.

Charles David Jenkins

MIRE FIRE!

'Twas the day - the farmer died
All about - his workers cried
Sobs galore - he did implore
Gather round - I must say more
When I'm gone - you'll move me on
To share the beauty - there outside
Please do this for me - when I have died
Came the time - although morose
When all came by - to move in close
Get my crossbow - from my den
Pluck a feather - from a hen
You might think I'm a simple dolt
Glue the feather to a bolt
Where falls the shaft - that I will fire
I would like to rest - when I do die
He shot - his plot - did go awry
It did not rise into the sky
He now does lie where bolt did fly
Alongside pigs in his old sty

John L Wright

THIS BAD HAIR DAY

My hair is like a fuzzball,
A brittle, rotten mess,
A pile of crazy corkscrews
Racing down my chest.

The dampness of the morning
Has taken its fatal toll.
The dew has kicked my head in,
The weather's scored its goal!

The frizz I see before me
Just makes me cry in grief.
I try a bit of shiny spray
Hoping for relief.

But nothing seems to work today,
My hair has no control,
The trouble is, this silly mop
Affects my mood and soul.

You see, I know I'll grouch and groan
And groan and grouch, not love,
Just because this covering
Has gone berserk above.

And once this 'thing' takes over
And rules me in my heart
It colours all I do and say
And joy and peace depart

There's nothing more depressing
For a woman in his way
Can her crowning glory
Overcome this bad hair day?

Judith Thomas

ANIMAL INSTINCTS

Stop thief! Said the magpie
Ney! Said the horse
You bitch! Said the cat
Cheeky! Said the monkey
Ass! Said the donkey
You sly old buggar! Said the fox
Forget it! Said the elephant
Coward! Said the chicken
Sycophants! Said the anteater
I'm cross! Said the zebra
Jump! Said the kangaroo
Roar! Said the lion
You heifer! Said the cow
Go home! Said the pigeon
Balls! Said the ball-frog
Balls! Said the parrot.

Paul Foreman

A HARD FACT

Jones was invited to tea with the boss,
During the meal he was at a loss.

The boss's wife's fruit cake and seed-cake were hard,
Poor Jones could masticate neither,
He surreptitiously passed them down to the dog,
Then found Spot couldn't manage them either!

Muriel Willa

I'M GETTING OLD!

When you're young and having fun
Life seems to be kind and not ready to run.
But as time goes by you start to see
Lots of little signs, your arm, elbow and knee,
They seem to be moving at a slower pace, as if in a different race.
You bend, you groan, you pull a funny face,
This never seemed to be a problem before
When you'd be the first out on the dance floor
Now it would take such an age, trip the light fantastic
Or come first in a race!
Is this how life is going to be?
All cod liver oil and suppositories!
Bed pans at dawn and wheelchair races
Go steady now I can still do my laces!
Lots of nights spent reminiscing,
Listening to stories that cause you to frown,
Yes that was me, I was that clown.

Angela Jones

BEN

His name is Ben,
He's not yet ten,
Black and white,
He's a beautiful sight,
With his bright white vest,
He's always looking his best,
He's never bad,
Or ever sad,
The mention of food,
And he's in a good mood,
When he's out for a run,
He's always having fun,
He will bring his ball,
Every time you call,
In his garden he likes to roam,
Seeking out a hidden bone.

Rebekah Jones (14)

MORE THAN MONEY CAN BUY

The best things in life are what I cannot touch
That to other people are not worth much
The memories I hold, the thoughts I treasure
That will remain with me forever and ever
And no matter how hard my life may get
I'll have these thoughts I won't forget
Of people I love and places I've been
What I've done and things I've seen
It doesn't matter what else is taken away
These memories I have will always stay.

Suzy Talbot

MY SQUARE WORLD

Around me, this world. My world. A square,
Framed and roofed by five surrounding squares.
Friendly and fun-filled this, my square world.

Within its warm and soft, supportive ground
I plant thought-seeds that sprout and grow,
Of all types and themes that make me glow.

I dream out my dreams from nine till five,
Then late at nights, and on sleepless dawns
In this wonder-world which is my square.

My square is flush with ungrowling shelves,
Cuddling books, files and films, pens,
Papers, trophies, snaps and puzzles-in-paint.

Time goes to sleep in my cosy square,
Hunger dies, thirst dries up, and thwarting
Pains never breathe. Gloom seldom blooms.

My square is my heaven, my carefree world
Of innocent bliss for my incensed soul
Where thoughts alone live and mind reigns.

My square. My world. My square world.

Kopan Mahadeva

LIGHT IN HIS DARKNESS

To wake and watch the golden dawn,
Creep across the dale,
To smell the good clear air,
To see the early birds wing,
Witness the hamlets shake off the night,
And slowly join this glorious day,
To reel in the knowledge,
That I am fit and active,
With a full part to play,
Then sadly to think of my neighbour,
Who would love to enjoy the same,
But he has been dealt a poor hand,
Housebound is he, locked away in his little box,
Anticipating my arrival,
To tell him of life over the hill,
Trivial insignificant tittle-tattle, tales,
Are his diet, his life-blood, his source,
Living and laughing off other people's escapades,
I can't help but think,
That one man's freedom of action,
Are paid for by another man's,
Pain, suffering and dissatisfaction.

P J Littlefield

SURFING THE WEB

Each night we go on the net
By courtesy of our PC
Around the world sometimes we go
Or send a few e-mails to people we know
The choice is endless whatever you want
Whatever you need, a click of the mouse
And it's there with all speed
No sitting and reading or watching the soaps
No time now, we are surfing, sorry folks.

Audrey Allott

FREE PAPER BRIGHTLINGSEA CHRONICLE

Please join with us and celebrate
Our one hundredth edition.
To bring you a free paper
Is our continuing mission.
We bring you lots of local news
And pay for it with ads,
A varied mix of stories
Is what the Chronicle has.
So if you have a story
Or a bit of news to share,
Contact your local Chronicle
And will try to print it there.
Keep sending in your adverts
And your tales of work and play
Hope you enjoy your Chronicle
The hundredth one today!

Norma Langley

NIKKI

She slumbers in her cosy bed
And I bend down to stroke her head . . .
Her silky coat as soft as down
Is glossy black and russet brown.

I love her funny little tricks
When 'fetching' balls and wooden sticks,
Her joyous bark when full of glee
And her tail that wags so merrily!

Her soulful eyes shine when I say
'Are we going for a walk today?'
Oh, lots of fun we have together
Going for walks despite the weather!

One autumn day all gold and mellow
When leaves were turning red and yellow,
Three wee puppies Nikki bore,
Just like their mother in miniature!

She tended them with loving care,
And so adorable they were!
Nature's miracle - Nikki's pride
In her babes she did not hide!

I am so glad I have my Nikki -
My darling dog, petite and pretty,
A true and treasured friend is she,
And such good company for me!

D Townshend

To Gilbert

Life began for you in Toulon
Where the mariners wear striped jerseys
Under their sailor collars and on
Their sleeves red anchor embroideries
To match the pom-poms on their hats.
Your lullaby was the music of the cicadas
And the Mediterranean. Your melodies with sharps and flats
Mimicked the cries of Provençal market vendors.
Trained in technique in Nice at the conservatoire
You imbibed the local aroma of saffron, thyme and sage.
As more and more songs were added to your repertoire
You jetted off from Orly. The world became your stage.
There were open air concerts in seaside gardens
And gala performances in vast auditoriums.
Your Opera of Aran was applauded by Parisians.
From Swiss chalets with potted geraniums
They came to listen to your midnight mass
But most will remember you in blue suit and spotted tie
Backed by musicians on drums, guitar and contrabass
Your hand cupped behind your ear if the pitch were too high.
You sang to us about a balloon seller,
A multicoloured bird, Nathalie in Moscow,
Buffoons, the rose and Monsieur Pointu from Canada.
We send our love and thanks, Bécaud.
Now it's adieu till we meet again.
Your memory lives on in tune and refrain.

Vivienne Brocklehurst

LITTLE TOM

Little Tom gives me such joy
My love I can't conceal
Although he thinks he's human
He's my golden cockateil.

He came to me so tiny and frail
With hardly a feather to be seen
Too weak to even feed himself
I thought he would surely fail.

Dear little Tom began to fight
He struggled to survive
With tender care day and night
Little Tom began to thrive.

Five years have passed, how Tom has grown
Feathers now a golden sheen
Bright red cheeks and yellow crown
The prettiest bird I've ever seen.

He comes and sits upon my hand
Nestles against my cheek
What pleasure this little bird gives
As he begins to speak.

He's repaid the time I cared for him
More than a hundred fold
Just so happy to be with me
My little bird of gold.

Pauline Nind

THE BEST THINGS IN LIFE

'I remember,' Maudie said,
'When bread was really bread.
And taste and texture were a must
And heaven was pinching half the crust.
When dripping cooked the weekend roast
And then was spread on Sunday toast.
Blackouts, rationing and more
When Mr Chamberlain went to war.
Air raid wardens, then the Yanks
Riding round our streets in tanks.
Tossing out with careless fun
Candy bars and chewing gum.

Gypsies selling wooden pegs,
Rubbing sand upon our legs,
Stockings were so hard to get,
As well as packs of cigarettes.
We queued for fruit, sugar, tea.
Potatoes, coal, in misery.
But oh the taste of yesteryear,
Roasted chestnuts, frothy beer.
The highs, the lows, a neighbour shared.
Every blessing, really cared!
And best of all, the great big fuss
When the boys came home to us.'

Margaret Marklew

I LIKE CATS

I like cats of all shapes and sizes,
When you belong to a cat, life's full of surprises.
I've known quite a few down the years, so it seems,
I even 'think cats' while asleep in my dreams.
I've known tigery striped ones, with brown velvet nose,
And nearly all white ones with pretty pink toes.
Cute black and white cats - black waistcoat, white socks,
The scrapes they get into, I've had a few shocks.
How I love young bright eyed cats, so eager to play,
And respect the old tired ones, that snooze all the day.
There are sharp faced Siamese cats and growly Burmese cats,
Ginger and white ones, black and all grey,
It's so hard to decide, which I like most of all,
Each one's so loveable, in its own special way.
I've known tiny short legged ones and huge overfed ones,
And some were as fierce as could be.
But when all's said and done, cats can be so much fun,
And I'm fairly convinced, that most cats like me.

Margaret Whitton

MY HEART BURNS FOR THE PENNINES

My heart burns for the Pennines,
Infusing with passion my beating blood,
There yearn, oh my stately pines,
Sprouting forth through cone and bud.

Just now the peaks are in thrall,
Subject to Jove's almighty wand;
While beaks and bills bid and call,
Diana de-robes by moorland pond.

King of the winds, Aeolus is blowing
Ruffling feathers and uprooting trees:
Singing hymns all nature's flowing,
Throbbing throstles dance I' the breeze.

Aloft in the air, falling flakes of snow
Kiss the cheek then deck the ground,
Crying, calling to all the lights below,
Oh come and seek the world around!

Heys Stuart Wolfenden

CORNWALL

Balmy breezes, whisper across, summer's prettiest coast
Endless golden sands, stretch, towards wondrous beach
Illusive gales hideaway legendary mythical ghosts
Slippery graggy rocks, meander far from reach
Handsome all mountains, ascending, rugged high
Embracing wild green valleys, sumptuous, lush, deep
Glistening oceanic waters, touch blue summer's sky
Catching sandy illusions where, pretty seashells sleep
Surfing while frothy foams, was tossing waves
Dancing ocean echoes, calmness calling for encore
She mourns Viking pirates, lonely coastal graves
Warm condensing seas, bathe creamy shingled shore
Capturing such beauty none could compare
With heaven's peaceful maiden, sweetest fair.

Ann Hathaway

BEST THINGS IN LIFE

The best things in your life are free,
There are glorious things to do and see,
The bluebells making a carpet so blue,
And the roses with colours of a different hue.
The freshly cut lawns, the budding trees,
And the wafting of that Heavenly breeze.
The buttercups and daisies which don't need tending,
The vision of such beauty, never-ending.
All these things that don't cost a thing,
Look at the pleasure it will always bring.
The flowers aren't always planted in rows,
The beauty of nature just grows and grows,
Just look around at the magnificent view,
Given as a gift, especially for you.

Edith Antrobus

A NATURAL GIFT

From me to you, I give,
The special gift to live.
Inside of me you grew,
I nurtured and cared for you.
You came from within me,
As I gaze lovingly,
I realise, now you've come,
You'll need me, coz I'm your mum.

Helen-Elaine Oliver (14)

SMALL THINGS

A raindrop glistens on a grateful leaf,
Its message is both pure and brief.
A butterfly alights and spreads its wings
Aglow with colours that the summer brings.
A thistle seed with soft, white hair
Floats in a gentle breath of air.
Amongst the grass, the pimpernels,
Gleam under crowds of scented bells
All as blue as distant skies.
A jaunty wren hunts tiny flies,
With tail acock, he shouts a song,
As flit, flit, flit, he darts along.
A squirrel searches in old leaves
For buried nuts he still believes
May lie unfound in autumn's stores.
Bees buzz busily, obeying special laws,
Whilst in the singing, sparkling streams
Elvers share Sargasso dreams,
And darting minnows play, before
The serious task of breeding more.
Everywhere these little things
Live for what each minute brings.

D Bruce

LOTTE'S COOKING

If you come to Iona
You'd have to be a loner
And not very inward-looking
To admit that your stay
Is not just to pass the time of day
But because
Of Lotte's cooking!

A few come because
St Columba landed
And stayed on
Cos he got stranded
For direction
He wasn't looking
He was fully lost until
He marched up Fairy Hill
And tasted -
Lotte's cooking!

Some come to the Abbey
And sit there
Getting flabby
Reciting prayers and petitions
All high follutin'
But although I sit and meditate
It's usually on the plate
Upon which is served -
Lotte's cooking!

The tourists come with cameras
Hats, macs and umbrellas
Not anticipated
At the time of booking
But all these things we do not need
There is only one important deed
To sit and taste
Lotte's cooking!

John Crowe

SILENCE OF THE BIRDS

All silent lie the busy birds that once adorned the bough and bower,
silent now at fall of night, silence of the early morning hour.

No lark ascending like a prayer now in the bright-blue sunlit sky,
swift fork-tailed swallows pause, no longer gorging on the wayward fly;
all these and more have sadly vanished, vanished with a tearful sigh.

Flight of the nightingale, no humble wrens, no robins front so red;
kingfisher's flash now memory, pert spotted mistle thrushes dead.

Winter's cold strips the trees, grips the birds; when spring arrives
what then?
Will long-tailed tits still flirt around the feathered skirts of the
shy blue hen?

Magpies, bold in their frockcoats, with cheeky starlings strut the lawn,
If they should go our world will be the poorer, quieter, more forlorn.

Grey heron that once stalked on stilts, surveyed the mossy river banks
along with avocets and curlews, rare and elegant greenshanks,
poor creatures, siphoning heavy metals, quicksilver, leached out lead;
effluents that spit pure poison mingle with the viscous river bed.

Competing supermarket owners force good farmers to cheap schemes;
do they care if birds and darting fish vanish from the poisoned streams?
At least their sleep is not disturbed by descants from our
much-loved birds,
by passing passerines whose notes trilled once in thrilling minor thirds.

No longer heard in crop-sprayed meadowlands or in the sheltering tree:
on their behalf I enter this anguished plea; let our feathered friends
fly free.
They are amongst the best things in life, a blessing beyond words,
it leaves a sad and empty feeling, this depressing silence of the birds

Norman Meadows

TRAINERS

The flick of a tick
On my trainers
Tells the world
I am cool,
No fool,
Walking on air,
Airing my style,
The queen of my street,
With crowns on my feet
Supporting my ego
And my sole.
The colour just right
The styling so neat
My feet
Have a treat
Every time I step out.
I love my trainers.

Barbara J Kerks

MY FAVOURITE PLACE

My garden is my delight,
In springtime it's a lovely sight,
Lawn and hedges neat and trim,
Borders bursting to the brim.

Shrubs and flowers vie for space
Creating such a perfect place:
Somewhere to sit and think and scheme
Somewhere to potter, rest or dream.

Many creatures come to play,
They brighten up the dullest day,
A rabbit peeps out from his hole,
A squirrel climbs the washing pole.

Hedgehogs forage for tasty grubs,
Birds adorn the flowering shrubs,
The wildlife is just fantastic,
What a shame they're only plastic.

Marilyn Wellman

FOR MY PRECIOUS PUSSY CAT
(Pussy-White-Paws)

My darling pussy cat
My ally and my greatest friend
Now I am here alone
When I am sad he always knows
He comes to sit upon my knee -
Then with his snow-white velvet paws
He paws my aching heart.
So I thank the unseen power
For his greatest gift to me -
My pussy cat, whose gentle purring
Brings sweet solace to my soul.

Marcella Pellow

THE HUNTING MIME

Desolate and barren is the moor,
As I sit and watch the kestrel soar.
Above the earth it hovers in air,
Looking for a rabbit or the long-eared hare.

Its presence portrayed in the evening light,
As dangerous as a tiger and as graceful as a kite.
Defying time for many a year,
Absorbing knowledge and dispensing fear.

Royalty of the food chain, their crown ensured,
Through starvation and disease the species endures.
So exiled to the moor until the end of time,
Constantly re-enacting the hunting mime.

Katie Johnson

MOMMY

Mommy, Mommy . . . tell me . . . where did I come from?
Was it from somewhere special, like your tum?
Will I get a little brother or sister at home?
As your front looks like the Millennium Dome?
Why does Daddy's hair now only grow on his chin?
because on his head, the hair there is so thin?
How does the sun move across the cloudy sky
and then turns into the moon, up there so high?
Every morning, why do I have to go to school?
to do everything teachers say, and obey their rules?
When Daddy drinks a lot, why can't he stand up?
is it some funny tea they put in the cup?
When I eat, why am I not supposed to speak?
Why do your bed springs squeak - two times a week?
Why do oranges and bananas all taste so fruity?
What do plain clothes policemen wear off duty?
Why does water go hard when it's cold and freezes
and when I try to eat it, I have lots of sneezes?
Why do you send me to bed, when I'm not sleepy?
Why do my lower parts sometimes get leaky?
Why do you get in a bad mood, once every month?
when Daddy says you do some very silly stunts?

Christopher Higgins

SOME THINGS THAT ARE FREE

The best things in life
Are the ones that are free
A smile from a child
A spring that is mild
A kiss in the dark
A walk in the park
A drop of rain when it's dry
An old worn out toy
You final degree
A waver of fee
A rose from a lover
And one from another
Freedom to roam
And to come back home
The first fall of snow
A friend when you're low
First prize in a race
Throwing the mace
A baby's first cry
A bird in the sky
The list now is ended
But it isn't done
There are plenty more things
That are free and great fun.

J Vessey

WHY TREES?

It's hard to define why
We like or love the things we do in life
It is all a mystery
I know I am attracted to the beauty of a tree
I love the ones that have a hollow
In which wise owls can sit
I love the details and complexities of the bark
Stained with green moss and fungi
I love the way strong branches reach high
Towards heaven, beyond the sky.
The gnarly knots, of deep roots, penetrating the earth.
I love the way a tree changes, throughout the year.
An endless story of rebirth.
It's hard to define why . . .

D P R

WILLETT THE PHILOSOPHER

It might be a hot summer day
With not a spare breath of air anywhere
We would sit in the cool shade
Just inside the cart shed
Or it might be winter by the open fire
Logs glowing red with comfort
It could even be a still mellow afternoon
In September digging potatoes on the plot
Behind the orchard where fruits hung ripe
And the warm soil turned sweet
Any such occasions were right for
My uncle Willett to become philosopher
And impress on me that the best things
In life are free.
A perfect sunset that on occasion would
Bring a tear of stirred emotion to the
Old man's eye at ease with all things natural
A dawn chorus with all its wonder and glory
Sliding by on time like the ribbon river
The cry of a new lamb or hoot of night owl
A young girl's laughter or sound of waterfall
Sound and silence movement and stillness
The old man loved the basic simple things of life
For to him these were the best things in life.

Clive Cornwall

THE GOSPEL SHIP

The gospel ship is sailing
Sailing to glory land
Won't you join the captain on that ship
Jesus is captain on that ship
Sailing o'er the sea of time

Fare is free upon that ship
All your needs supplied
Insurance guaranteed on that ship
Passengers wanted now.

The gospel ship will soon be full
Sailing the perilous sea of time
Won't you obey the captain's call
Come, come now
Lest you hear the captain's call
'Where, where art thou'
Gospel ship is sailing
Sailing the sea of time
Won't you join the captain
On that fair ship, time of sailing's now.

To lose one's wealth is much
To lose one's health is more
To lose one's soul is such a loss
No one can restore.

Frances Gibson

SHE IS SIMPLY THE BEST

The best thing in my life, has got to be my mum,
With her constant care and love, she is my number one,
Sharing all the good times, sharing all the bad,
Laughing with me when I am happy,
Comforting me when I am sad,
She is the firm foundations, on which I build my life,
And with her by my side, I can cope with any strife,
She is my lifelong friend, and so much more,
And there will never be another,
Who can shape my life, and touch my heart,
As my very own dear mother.

Clare Allen

HONEY BUN

Fiddle-de-dee
isn't life funny
but there's nothing
I like better
than a nice jar of honey -

Mum caught me once
with finger in jar -
she said 'Watch it
young lady or I
might tell your pa'.

I said 'Come off it Mum -
he'd just think it funny,
for there's nothing
he likes better
than a nice jar of honey!'

Mary Skelton

A LITTLE GENTLEMAN IN MY LIFE

A hand to hold
A tear to wipe
My life starts from you left to right.

Embrace you
Love you until I am no more.

We shall learn the magic of life together
Yes, you are my little gentleman.

Parveen K Saini

CUCKMERE'S MOMENT

The whispering wind passed gently by,
Causing ripples on the river, to murmur and sigh,
The sun with its beams, warmed the fresh air
Reality of make belief, relaxed,
Without a shadow of care . . .

Swans pass by, with such leisurely grace,
Dignified movements, in time honoured pace.
This magical moment, seems plucked from time,
Life is a gift, displaying this significant sign.
Watching in awe, content to see,
Meandering, drifting, life's luxury free . . .

We as mere mortals, it's pleasure indeed,
Autumnal's mystery, gratefully received,
Arms outstretched, embracing the sun,
Welcoming autumn, it's just begun.
Blending of colours, riches of gold,
Add to perfection, this season beholds,
Enjoying this gift, on a warm sunny day,
Fulfilling contentment, of spiritual thanks,
Gratefully conveyed . . .

Lorna Tippett

MY FRESHY MADE BED

Upstairs, I rejuvenate myself
Laid on my plumped and cushioned bed,
Comfortably soft are my pillows
Where all my cares I shed,
Resting on my soft mattress
Covered with eider quilt,
So cosy, after my warm bath
In laziness, I wilt.
In luxury and richness
All my tired senses meet,
My naked body bathes in freshness
Between, eider quilt and sheet.
Silky are the clean covers
A garden's perfume fills my room,
I can smell relaxing lavender
And scent from roses in full bloom,
I merge, I mingle,
My bed is now an utter pleasure,
With fresh perfume, on air,
I may drift to sleep,
Quietly, at my leisure.

Susan Carole Roberts

GLORY OF THE HILLS

Up on the downs
Skylarks sing and fly,
This special place
Where ground touches sky.
Trees guard like sentries
Windswept but proud,
Watching the skyline
Sometimes lost in cloud.
The air is fresh
Life stands still,
Just standing and looking
Gives such a thrill.
Sometimes it's quiet
Tranquil and warm,
On other occasions
A full blown storm.
Across the horizon
There is very little built,
Just hedges and fields
In a patchwork quilt.
These wonderful hills
This wide open space,
This little bit of England
A heavenly place.

Derk Pile

BEST THINGS IN LIFE

I have a very special gift
I often think about it through the day
My gift is something special
One I cannot give away.

I found I had my special gift
When I was taught to read and write
I loved to practice all I learned
And I read every poetry book in sight.

I tried to write a poem
Practised hard for it to rhyme
If I couldn't find the perfect words
I would try just one more time.

I might not be too good at it
But I love it just the same
It's wonderful to open a poetry book
And sometimes read my name.

I am not a Shakespeare
Or a Wordsworth this is true
But I hope when you read my poems
They will stir something inside you too.

Pauline Drew

FRENCH WINDOWS AND RAILINGS

Simple ideas are the best,
Changing people's opinions,
If only you knew what's yet *unseen,*
You'd flip your lid, and become keen.

There's more to life in the *'unseen',*
Standing by the 'window' in your mind,
The *'way'* to there is *'truth'* and *'life',*
Follow the path - husband and wife!

Single people, young and old,
Healthy, wealthy, sick or poor,
Workers, students, unemployed,
Let fresh air enter your mind!

The *outside* world's invited in,
When open doors allow 'enter',
Fresh air replaces still stale air,
Which was *OK* until right now.

Stale air's replaced by all that's *new,*
The railings keep the children safe,
The view's better than those four walls,
Especially during the daylight.

No matter which level you're at,
You'll welcome *garden* in your flat,
Just open up and you can see,
Ground floor - *flowered* scenery.

D Sawyer

BLESSED IS THE LIFE YOU LIVE

Life is not so hard to live,
when love is always there to give

When friendly words can lift despair,
or just a touch to know you're there.

When hands you hold, that they won't
fall, or when you run to heed a call.

When a tender look can light the day,
or a loving smile can stem the grey.

When a single kiss can mend a heart,
or arms that hold, no more to part.

When you walk into a lonely room, and
the lonely smile, and begin to bloom.

Should these gifts you freely give, then
blessed are you, for the life you live.

Jim Cuthbert

FOR OUR LOVE OF TREVOR!

For our love of Trevor,
And a beautiful life.
To ease the pain,
And ease the strife!
Why can't you be good,
Like you know you should?
Giving us love,
Like you know you could!

Perhaps today,
You will meet Trevor!
Let him into your life,
Let him live forever!
He's a beautiful person,
With a beautiful mind.
Live like Trevor,
And see what you find!

There would be,
So much happiness,
Happiness to share!
Love for one another,
Love to show you care!

Live like Trevor,
And you will see,
Just how wonderful,
Life can be!

Graham Mitchell & Amy Kelly

AT THE HAIRDRESSERS

I visited a salon, the place that does my hair,
You hear some funny stories as you're sitting in the chair.

A lady came to have a perm, dressed in a real fur coat,
A hat to match the coat you know, an assistant she did note.

'I did have matching mitten but alas I think they're lost,'
She looked a little worried, perhaps thinking of the cost.

'Take your hat and coat off and do please take a seat,
When I've finished with your hair madam, your perm will be so neat.'

Imagine the surprise she had when taking off her hat,
As she glanced into the mirror, on her head the mittens sat.

'I really feel quite silly,' said the lady going red,
'I thought I'd lost my mittens and they're sitting on my head.'

She thought for just a moment, to think how they got there,
She'd tucked them in her hat back home and now she'd found the pair.

Betty Hattersley

A Poetic 'Genius' Sees The Funny Side

A place I will not earn
Within the hall of fame,
Among poetic geniuses
I will not find acclaim,
Parnassus coveted heights
I could not hope to scale
And to vie with
The literary greats,
I know that I would fail.
Perhaps I lack the brilliance
That gift unique and style,
Even though I wield my pen
And write once in a while,
Just about the ordinary things
That make the daily grind,
The pleasantries and kindness
Uplifting to the mind.
Special moments savouring,
Friendship's abiding worth,
Each dawning that brings
Its hopes anew
To the awakening earth.
Though in literary spheres
My work may not excel,
But when I read it
I feel pleased
And have a laugh as well.

Brigid Smith

I REMEMBER

What was her name?
  I must not guess!
I call her Mame,
  For it was - Jess!

She had red hair,
  As she was blonde!
We met up there,
  Down by the pond!

Her smile was sweet,
  She wore a frown!
And looked petite,
  In her green gown!

She stood erect,
  And as she sat,
A dog passed by,
  A lovely cat!

He first remarks,
  Were light and gay;
Her dainty mouth,
  Had nought to say!

Her sandals green,
  A brilliant blue!
Her tiny feet,
  Had lost a shoe!

The May sun shone,
  That cold December!
I'm almost sure now
  I remember!

R Bissett

DOG TRAIN AFTERNOON

Rough, rough
Fluff and stuff
On the dog train this afternoon

Dogs in baskets
Dogs on leads
Dogs in rucksacks
If you please

Rough, rough
Tough's tough
On the dog train this afternoon

Comb and groom
'Yappity-yap'
Paws on floors
'Mind your back!'

Rough, rough
It could be 'Crufts'
On the dog train this afternoon

Dogs in pockets
Dogs on string
Tails in corridors
Wag and swing

Rough, rough
Enough's enough!

It's a dog train afternoon

Jane Phillimore

CHILDHOOD TRIPS

'I spy' we played, travelling in the back of the car
Continually asking Dad 'How far?'
The scenic route was very calming
Not the horrific town sights that are so alarming
Breaking the long journey
In a lay-by we'd rest:
We'd put our parents memories to the test
Did they pack the kettle . . .
The water and cups as well?
The Calor gas stove gives a wonderful smell
Nothing tastes better than a cup of tea . . .
Out in the open air for passers-by to see!
Then into the woods - the bracken we'd tread
Feeling the fresh country air
Floating around our heads:
Searching and searching until we find
Somewhere we can squat our little behind:
Because all this tea in the open air
Leaves us cross legged and in despair . . .
                                        Ah! Heaven

Julie Powell (nee Carter)

ALL WE LIKE HEBRIDES

Da Da Da-Da Da Da
Da Da Da-Da Da Da . . .
I waft the biro baton
To the direction
Of
The four elements
On the upturned bucket bottom
The hastily-gathered orchestra
Responds
Non-rehearsed
As one man
Ba Ba Ba-Ba Ba Ba
Ba Ba Ba-Ba Ba Ba
One by one
The audience edges forward
To the platform
To get a listen-see
Fingal's caves wide open!

John Crowe

THE SUN

This morning the sun shone on our faces
Warming our flitting dreams as we woke.

It shone on our eyes and with golden surprise
On the shining words as we spoke.

It illuminated our charms. Warmed up our arms
And its light dappled the eiderdown.

Well . . .
    Actually . . .

The sun shone on my face this morning
And bored its light in my eye.
It showed up the dust and shone on the rust
Of my jewellery from days gone by.
It faded the curtains and carpet.
Prevented me getting my sleep.
But what can I say? It's here every day
And it doesn't do any good to weep!

Maureen Thomas

TWO PRETTY PUSSY CATS

I've got two pretty little pussy cats.
They mean the world to me.
And when they jump upon my knee
They are as jealous as can be.
Now Storm is smoky grey and white.
As pretty as a picture is she.
Then Tickles is just black and white
As handsome as can be.

Helen Barwood

A SINKING FEELING

My first year of teaching, I can look back and smile
A time for asserting my own teaching style.
Our history component was the Titanic's fate
So the release of the film at that time was just great
The film had inspired, given food for thought.
Their quest for knowledge it really had caught.
We had looked at Primary and Secondary Source,
And placed events in a time-line as part of the course.
We had spent many a week to compare and contrast
The film had given them a good sense of the past
So imagine my dismay when I encountered the blip
A voice enquired 'Did Celine Dion go down with the ship?'

Nicky Chaperlin

COMING AND GOING

When you're driving to the city,
Looking forward to the stores,
How it seems an awful pity
Other cars are out in scores!
Every traffic light you come to
Is sure to be on red,
So of course, the air has turned blue
With what some drivers said!
Then it seems that every roadway
Is needing some repair,
By the time we reach a broad way
We'll all have greying hair!
But coming home is faster . . .
There's a calmness in the lanes;
No traffic jam disaster,
No roadworks causing pains.
We look forward to coming and going,
Yet travelling is surely a mess.
All we get from this to-ing and fro-ing
Is a whole lot of worry and stress!
Don't go round the bend
When you reach journey's end, my friend.

Evelyn Balmain

A PG TIP

Never treat a chimpanzee
To a cup of tea;
Though you see them on your tellies
Sipping cuppas in green wellies,
In reality the truth
Is slightly more uncouth -
They'll forget what they've been taught
And just treat all as sport,
They'll put the saucers on their heads
And bounce high upon their beds,
Sending cakes and tea sets reeling
As they decorate the ceiling;
So I think that you'd agree
That it would be a tragedy
To give a chimpanzee
A cup of tea!

Martin Winbolt-Lewis

STRANGE HAPPENINGS

Fifty cats in scarlet hats
went chasing after twenty rats.
But on reaching Bristol town
their purple socks came falling down.

A dog inhabited by a hundred fleas
considered himself the bee's knees.
Until his occupants upped and went
without paying any weekly rent.

Six Chinese men with emerald eyes
went out fishing for giant meat pies.
A monstrous crocodile at once arose,
swallowing them except their toes.

An old lady walking the strand
consumed a huge rubber band.
As she hiccuped she bounced up and down
All over the streets of London town.

Terry Burrows

SMILES AND LAUGHTER

A smile changes your features if only for a little while,
it can make your eyes sparkle, so go on give us a smile.
it's that little something that cost you nothing;
You can take it with you wherever you go.
You can never leave your smile at home,
So just smile and say hello.

It takes more mussel energy to frown, than it does to smile,
so do yourself a favour and smile for a while.
Two horses walk into a pub and the barman says,
'Why the long faces' Well no one told us it was happy hour!

Well, will you look at that we almost made you smile,
I bet it was quite painless and now you're trying hard
not to laugh. Well go on and treat yourself,
have a good chuckle on us.

Laughter can be quite contagious, so why not give a try.
It helps lighten up your day, and it's one thing the
government can't tax. So bring some laughter back into
your day, and it will help to make the world a better place
if we take time to laugh and smile with those we really love.

And if by chance we meet a stranger on the street
and their eyes you see a smile don't forget to smile back.

Robert Waggitt

Diva At The Village Dance

Dressed up to kill looking like a diva,
Entr'ing the room, men worked up a fever,
Strutted the dance floor in sexy split skirt,
Game old Mick had to unbutton his shirt!
Slinked up to the stage to chat up the bass
She tripped on a step, fell flat on her face.

Jill I Henderson

PROBEVERBS

Opinions are like noses
Everybody has one
Yet, each has its own smell
A bird in hand
Will fly away to the bush
Because it's safe there
He who laughs best
Is really enjoying the show
And would always laugh last
When the cat is away
The mouse would play
Because it is his day
Dance like a butterfly
And sting like a bee
And hide like a rat
Speak up, be heard
Speech is silvern, silence
Not golden, it means consent
A cat may look at a king
If it is real hungry
If not, the mouse is safe
A hungry man is an angry man
Man is not only stomach
After eating, don't irritate him
Who made all those proverbs
Early to bed, let's debate that quote
Makes man wealthy, wise and remote

Ato Ulzen-Appiah

DUCKS OF CUERDEN PARK

Quack, quack. Quack quack!
I welcome you today, sir.
If I were a cat
I would certainly purr.

My friends and I saw your dog
who came down the path with friendly tread.
We waited and watched until you came
with your usual pack of bread.

We have gathered round your feet
with upturned beaks and bright eyes.
We have fought, chased and pecked our fellows,
contrary to your desires.

Quack, quack! Oh sir, you have not
fed me my fair share.
I have pecked at the bag and your shoes
to indicate my plight and despair.

Dear sir, you are so kind
to remedy this oversight.
With autumn's chill winds, your bread
will warm me through another night.

Robert Allen

A PAWN IN THE GAME

It's no life at all as a pawn
Sometimes I feel so forlorn
It's alright for a knight
He can stand up and fight
But it's no life at all as a pawn

 How I envy the freedom of the castle
 He can move up and down, lucky rascal
 And the bishop can roam
 In one leap far from home
 I'd rather be a bishop or a castle

I worship the king and his queen
They have a regal air so serene
But he'll meet a gory fate
If he persists with his Czech mate
For they say that man from Prague is a fiend

 It's no life at all as a pawn
 But I could soon be reborn
 If I get to the end square
 I can become a new piece there
 Then I'll go round and round like a storm
 And make life hell for the other side's lowly pawns

Stuart Delvin

GETTING DRESSED

My feet are both down one knicker leg,
My jumper's inside out
And back to front, coat's upside down
But what's all the fuss about?

So what if my right shoe's on my left foot,
My buttons done up wrong?
You said to hurry and get dressed
And it didn't take *that* long!

Catherine Champion

BEST NIGHT OUT

I'd just dyed my hair
A lovely shade of blonde
I thought I looked gorgeous
I was getting looks all around

I thought it must be right what people say
Blondes have more fun
So many admiring looks were coming my way

I stood at the bar
Feeling all beautiful and gay
When a beautiful young man started coming my way

He tapped me on the shoulder
And whispered into my ear
'Your skirt's tucked in your knickers
And we can all see your rear.'

*Aaaah! *****! . . . Noooo.*

J Gatenby

GOOD ADVICE

When my uncle was two
A new baby was due
'Twas my mother so anxious to 'foller'.
Granny lay on the floor
The midwife at the door
Cried 'Do ee bide still, and don't holler!'

In most family life
There's some trouble and strife
And we all get hot under the collar,
So as time has gone by
We have oft raised the cry
'Now, do ee bide still and don't holler!'

When the car will not go
When there's two feet of snow
And a power cut, you bet your last dollar
Don't shout, stamp and frown
Remember Nurse Brown
And 'Do ee bide still and don't holler!'

Jean Saunders

HOTEL POOL

Come on in, the water's lovely;
It's warm but yet not too much so.
You'll wish you had if the weather changes
And maybe starts to rain and blow.

Come on in, the water's lovely;
It'll do you good without a doubt.
You know they said to exercise,
Otherwise you'll remain quite stout.

Come on in, the water's lovely;
Ignore the bits of floating things.
Everyone else isn't being so fussy;
Here, use this pair of water wings.

Come on in the water's lovely;
Best to use your sandals, though,
Then the rubble on the bottom
Won't infect your poor sore toe.

Wendy Kirkpatrick

Out Of The Mouths . . .

I heard this tale the other day about a child in Sunday school
Who was told the story of Moses and then asked to draw
the part of the story she thought she saw.

Of baby, basket and bulrushes,
A lovely picture Jenny handed in
The story of Moses with skyscrapers, tall and thin.

The teacher praised the little girl
And asked, 'What are these buildings, Jenny Earl?'
'They are the banks of the Nile!'
Jenny replied with a smile.

Susan Wilson

KISS

He forgot tadpoles,
the hunt for lost gold
and his vow of never,

never-ever speaking
to a girl with teeth braces.
When she said

she'd show him
how grown-ups kiss.
Later, he blamed

a school bully
for his bruised lip.

Les Merton

IT COMES TO US ALL

Sooner or later it comes to us all,
Old age creeps on, our energies pall.
Actions are slow, our memory goes,
Our interests fade as we sit and doze.

Our hands won't do what we want them to do,
Our legs won't go where we want them to go.
Our limbs are stiff and so full of pain
We get up, then want to lie down again.

We diet and exercise then take our pills
The ones supposed to cure all our ills!
We're given advice, don't stick in a groove
Go out and walk, just keep on the move.

But we are so tired and feeling so rough
We just want to rest for we've had enough.
We go to the doctor and he with respect
Says you're getting on, what do you expect!

So all you young folk, look after your health
Don't worry and fret to accumulate wealth.
Growing old is hard work, look after your bone
Old age creeps on and it don't come alone!

We old ones go on and stay close to God
He'll see us through as onward we plod.
For he has His plan for each one and all
When He is ready He'll give us a call.

When that day comes from pain we'll be free!
We'll skip and we'll dance through eternity!
Sooner or later it comes to us all
Take heed, be ready, respond to His call.

Beryl R Daintree

I Am A Poet - But I Didn't Know It

All this time
I was trying to rhyme

My lines lacked sense
And I just got tense

The large blank page
Increased my rage

I could only stare
At the pure white glare

And juggle with the riddle
Of writing words in the middle

The poem after this heroic task
Was as good as one could ask

My fingers crossed in hope
I popped it in an envelope

Now to post it without delay
At last my poem can wing its way

The postman's feet
Keep the beat

Leaflets and pamphlets
To deliver to flatlets

A poem to Peterborough
From a poet so thorough

The winning entry
Of the century

But if it rains I'm out of luck
As my stamps will become unstuck

All the words have now been wrung
From a budding poet who's as yet unsung

Derek Harvey

NOSES

Noses are such funny things they decorate your face
I wonder who decided they should go in such a place
Was it just to hold in place, the surplus of your skin
Or was it that there was no room in which to squeeze it in?

Why then does it have to be; an awkward piece of flesh.
I suppose if it was flattened, it would really look a mess
Just like a pancake on your face that spreads from cheek to cheek
and if you never had it, would you be able to speak

I suppose when all is said and done it tidies you up quite well
It's useful when there's food about to savour up the smell
But sometimes you will find that you wished you never had
a really good and sensitive nose when things around smelt bad

E M Budge

FROZEN STIFF

A hard frost and ice covered the land
The garden pool was frozen over
My husband inspected what lay outside
I said 'Look out for my frog called Croaker'

He came in and said in a solemn voice
'The frog was frozen to the bottom
I've removed the ice he looks alright
Only time will tell if he goes rotten'

Alarmed and dismayed I cried 'Is he dead?'
My husband looked puzzled and replied
'I don't think that he was ever alive
He's made of concrete or stone' he sighed.

Gillian Mullett

THE FLY

As I entered the café,
I heard the 'buzz' of a fly.
I just simply ignored it,
And ordered my Shepherd's pie.

I was enjoying my meal,
When the fly intervened,
It was there . . . on my plate,
Eating my green runner beans.

I rolled up my paper,
Gave the fly such a slap
And my pie finished up
In this big workman's lap.

I said, 'I'm ever so sorry'
As I scraped away the pie.
But he hadn't any manners,
And he punched me in the eye.

As I staggered to the door
I knocked a man coming in.
He thought I was attacking him,
So he kicked me in the shin.

The owner of the café,
Shouted abuse I can't repeat.
Then grabbed me round the throat,
And hurled me into the street.

As I lay on the pavement,
Trying hard not to cry,
Something landed on my nose,
It was that horrid little fly.

Dennis Young

A FOOL'S PARADISE

She led him down a country lane
The sun was at its height
He asked her what her name was
she said 'Miss Dynamite'

She certainly looked the part an' all
Her figure was tremendous
She wore a short skirt up to her knees
Stockinged black suspenders

She led him up the garden path
Amongst the flowers would linger
Along with his engagement ring
she'd twist him round her finger!

She said indeed she loved him
Her love would never falter
If he would buy her a house and car
They would soon be at the altar

He gambled here, borrowed there
He really felt quite harried
To give her all the things she craved
It turned out she were married!

T A Eady

IT'S FUN

It's naughty, but it's fun
November 4th is here again.
Mischievous night rears its head
Now what, oh what can we do.

Guy Fawkes was a man of many parts
What did he nearly lead us to?
A very different world,
One we are grateful we did not see.

Now what are we doing on Mischievous night?
We knock on a few doors and run away.
We hide behind the wall
Naughty but ever so funny.

Last year I got a thick ear from my dad,
What on earth did I do?
I knocked the bucket of food for the pigs,
Right through our back door
And then I ran away.

Even my friends didn't want to know
Oh it was so funny,
Naughty - but ever so funny.

Janet Cavill

OUR VICAR

We have a fine vicar called John
Now promoted to be a can-on.
The power of his fire
Now goes further and higher
Than e'er it had previously gone.

'Twas sad at the end of one year
That his voice became weak and unclear.
He went to the Doc
Who said, 'Do not talk,
Or your voice, it could quite disappear.'

This canon, whose surname is Hughes,
Would like to dispense with the pews.
So hearing him preach
That God's love is for each
Is not the only good news!

His curates - they must have no life -
Departures are suddenly rife.
Poor John bears a load
But he's just cracked the code -
And now appoints husband *and* wife.

He's been with us now a decade
And to him our due debt must be paid.
Don't take him for granted
Or he may be planted
Elsewhere - or a bishop be made.

To us, John, it's simple and clear
That you with your wife, Annie, dear
Should stay with us longer
And help us grow stronger -
So here's to the next ten year.

David Varley

COLOURFUL CHARACTERS

The King while out hunting last week
Fell from his horse with a shriek.
He landed on tussocks,
Grass speared his buttocks,
His future looks awfully bleak.

The prince surfed the net one wet day.
I walked by and heard him say
'My word what a website.
That pair, what a fine sight!
I'd like us to meet come what may.'

As Lady Letitia went out
She thought she heard her husband shout.
She paid no attention,
Thought anal retention
While the poor man choked on a sprout.

The Countess out shopping in town
Quite suddenly started to frown.
Her bra strap had snapped,
For cash she was strapped,
Then felt her new wait slip fall down.

The circuit judge Sir Arthur Hunt
Could often be awfully blunt.
To the man in the dock
Said 'You're in for a shock.
Just look at the marks down your front.'

The butler arrived late for work.
The maid thought he was a right burk.
But soon she discovered
The Queen quite uncovered
In bed wearing only a smirk.

Catherine Craft

PHENOMENON FATIGUE

I'm sick and tired of Harry Potter
A brilliant boy I'm sure, but not a
Patch on jolly Billy Bunter:
(Classic books you'll have to 'hunt-fer')
Media hype today is endless,
Parents would prefer to spend less:
Accept this cult, and come what may,
Harry P is here to stay.

Corinne Lovell

A CHOCOLATE CAKE

A chocolate cake and I came in
to place upon a table therein
but a mishap fell upon the way
which amused my guests of the day
the chocolate cake it slid off the plate
and met the carpet for a tasty date
I calmly gathered the cake up off the floor
and proceeded to the table once more
and there it sat none much the worse
and this is the end of my humorous verse.

Patricia A Taylor

ONE MAN AND HIS DOG

I watched a stranger walk up to a man and his dog,
'A magnificent hound! Remarked stranger; Does he bite?'

'Not to my knowledge!' the overheard dialogue,

The dog-lover stroked and patted the Mastiff in delight,
Whereupon the dog sunk his teeth into the admirer's arm,
Stepping back in alarm,
The Mastiff fan said, 'You told me he didn't bite!'
'He certainly did me harm!'

Replied the man, 'Don't pick a quarrel with me mate, it's not my fight!
'He's not my dog!'

Hilary Jill Robson

'SEXTY' YEARS YOUNG!
(On A Male Reaching Sixty Years)

You've reached the age of 'sexty'
You've done the 'bloomin' lot'
Occasionally you're 'testy'
But often times you're not!

You've travelled all the highways,
On English soil and foreign
To keep abreast of northern ways,
You've even got a 'sporran'.

You've lingered on the continent,
Abroad you're not a 'rooky'
And we hope you've been content
To keep away from 'nooky'!

You've reached the age known as mature!
The age of sensibility,
And tho' your jog is somewhat slower
No doubt of your virility.

Teenage girls sigh when you're near
You take it in your stride,
You know you're safer with a beer
Than going for a 'ride'

The years have just enhanced your charms
Old friends can verify,
And if you'll only 'grease their palms'
They'll even tell a lie!

You've learned the value of a real good meal
So give the 'chicks' the 'bird'
For keeping on an even keel
Stick to your *'old crossword'!*

Doreen M Carne

THE THRILL OF THE TWILIGHT YEARS

Ageism is a form of prejudice
At seventy we're not over the hill
Though perhaps we take life steadier
And it takes longer to achieve a thrill

Having zimmer races, to the post office
- On pension day - is a jolly good form of exercise
To keep arthritis at bay
Some are full of energy at seventy
They hike and join rambling clubs
Other folk at seventy
Crawl around the pubs

They jet away to warmer climes
It's surprising where they've gone
White water rafting in Canada
And trekkin' in Napal
And some cruise the Mediterranean
On a manhunt I recall!

On a ship there's a captive audience
Their conquests can't run far!
So the merry widow pursues her conquest
Under a wandering star

Old fiddles can play a wonderful tune
Romance can blossom by the silvery moon
They say in the end you're as young as you feel
And positive thoughts are always ideal

Anthony J Gibson

CREATIVE WRITING CLASS 1-4-2000

Said Ms Pauline Kirk,
Suppressing a smirk,
'I want you to write a good poem.
It mustn't have a beginning
Nor even an end,
The middle must be very short,
And it must be sent
To 6 Letsby Avenue,
Down the road by
The old 'Bull and Bush'.
Absolutely no rush!
The prize is five figure,
They don't come much bigger,
I wish you all the best!'

After that there was laughter,
We thought nothing could be dafter,
Seeing it as April Fool jest!

Richard Birch

THOSE PEOPLE

Those people there, a funny lot, to say the least,
I mean, for instance, going down the road, today,
They stopped me, and asked what I was doing,
What am I doing? I said,
Can't you see, I'm walking to the station,
If I don't hurry up, I will miss the train,
Nonsense they said, the train won't be in
For quite a while yet,
In fact, we're going on it as well,
As well as what? I asked, same as you, silly head,
Think to myself, it's going to be one of those days,
I can tell, and it's not even twelve o'clock,
Got out right side of bed this morning
So it's not that, or anything else,
I ate my breakfast OK, nothing wrong there
It must be Saturday, when I thought, I was going to work,
And you see, I don't work Saturdays,
Oh dear, I am a silly so and so,
Have just remembered, of course it's Saturday,
That's why I have all these whistles, scarf and big hat on,
Our team is playing away,
I don't know, what's got into me, lately,
I'm sure those people thought, now isn't he a silly clot,
Doesn't know what day it is,
And can't see that we're all going to football,
Our team would need to win after all this,
Or I'll never live it down,
Imagine asking someone, dressed as referee and linesman,
Where they are going
Ah well, better times tomorrow I hope.

Hugh Campbell

BEES WITH FLEAS!

Whoever said that 'Bees
Are completely riddled with fleas?'
Now was it you?
It can't be true -
You're such a terrible tease!

Kerri Fordham

ANYTHING BUT THAT!

He has a collection of Valentine cards,
  that he's sent or received over the years,
One particular pair caught my eye had
  me laughing close to tears.

It seems he met this widow on our local
  cliffs as both walked their dogs,
They did this walk every day, in all kinds
  of weather, in sunshine or in fogs.
It seems she told him, not once had she ever
  received a Valentine card,
This was the verse, that he then sent her,
  for he was the local bard.
Last night as I lay sleeping dreaming
  of Yuletide logs,
I dreamt you came into my room all
  alone without your dogs,
As I went to embrace you,
  suddenly you moved out of reach,
So don't put up a fight meet me tonight
  alone on Minster beach.
What he didn't realise was, that she too
  was a local bard,
So when he received her reply it hit
  him really hard,

I went down to Minster beach last night
and waited for you in the pale moonlight,
All alone feeling blue, hours in the cold
just waiting for you,
Finally I went home and cuddled my dogs
so just you stuff your flaming logs!

Fred Grimwade

BLIND DATE

The duchess was a dragon,
Feared by all reporters,
Ramrod-straight, sarcastic
Yet she had lovely daughters!

She ate the press for breakfast,
Lunched vinegar and glass,
Was famous throughout Britain
As a racist upper class.

Interviews were fearsome
Yet I tried my luck.
When granted an audition,
My colleagues praised my pluck.

She glared across the table
As I took the other side
I swear that I was shaking . . .
'Great meeting you' I lied.

To right and left her girls sat,
Like two roses by a thorn,
They smiled at me so sweetly
With ardour I was torn.

The prettier, upon the left
Touched my knee with trepidation
Emboldened I passed her a note
Making an assignation.

I waited trembling 'neath the stairs
In darkness came my lover,
I kissed her hard, the light came on . . .
My God . . . It was her mother!

Sarah Blackmore

GRAY AND DEBBO ON HONEYMOON

Gray and Debbo on honeymoon
On the twenty-first day of June
On the beach on Ibiza
They were prouder than Caesar
Making magic 'neath a silver moon

At a restaurant for their tea
Debbo asks the waiter slowly
For 'uncooked squid for my gran
Also weewee and spam
And a burnt bull's belly for me'

Then Gray a Spanish export in kind
Said 'Seafood salad for my Debbo so kind
Two pints of Fosters
Ham sandwich from the Costas
And a belly steak well done no rind

H G Griffiths

A WEEDY LIMERICK

There was a young housewife from Leeds,
Whose garden was full of tall weeds:
She wanted sweet flowers
And fragrant bowers,
But she sowed all the wrong sorts of seeds.

Roma Davies

A Limerick

There was an
old man
called Reg
who smelled
of rotten veg

The smell
was so bad
he was branded
a cad
That smelly
old man
called Reg.

P Allen

OUR MAVIS AND HER FELLA

Mavis, our kid, was mad keen on this fella named Ken,
He were a bit of a puny lad, but not bad looking.

Anyway, the first time they went to bed together,
Poor Ken fell out and rolled away.
Mavis having a big heart
And not wanting to embarrass the poor lad,
Gently called 'Ooh! Ken wherever have you got to?'

Ken, being a bit of a wimp,
Didn't answer and just lay there.
Mavis thought he must be asleep
And thus they remained all night.

Come mornin', Ken tried to creep out,
But our kid spied him
And gently called 'Don't fret Ken luv,
Never mind, we'll try again Thursdee.'

G Livermore

LITTLE HYENA

The moon shone so bright,
you could hardly believe it was night.
But you should have seen Tina,
the little hyena,
as she jumped up and down with delight.

Martin Snowdon

JANUARY SALES

It's January sales
and what a delight,
to pick up a bargain -
knocked down, overnight.
'Armani' suits
with half price stickers,
just slung on the rail -
next to thermal knickers.
Sparkly blouses
cut low at the chest -
but when it's freezing
wear a thick vest.
Some queue outside,
looking cold and bored.
Last year someone died -
frozen to the road.
But hurry, make haste,
head for your store -
It's January sales, yes,
bargains galore.

Ken Price

VENUS DE MILO

Venus De Milo ain't got no arms,
But she has other plentiful charms,
My one and only regret,
Is that she is an Alabaster statuette,
I long to give her a kiss and cuddle,
But her lack of limbs leave me in a muddle,
I only want her to hold my hand
But she doesn't seem to understand,
She gives me scornful reprimand
There she stands upon her shelf,
Making a proper exhibition of herself,
How on earth does she eat a banana,
Put her curlers in,
Or tie a bandanna?
Smoke a fag or a Havana,
it must have been a woeful day,
When the sculptor missed his clay,
And made an unsightly slip,
And broke off her arms at the hip,
I've heard of a chip off the old block,
Alas poor Venus got a shock,
Without arms she must stay,
My idol with the feet of clay.

Alan Pow

BREEZY BRUMMIE

A girl from out Birmingham way,
Decided she needed to play.
So she dropped to her knees,
And started a breeze,
By trumping for more than a day.

Geoffrey Woodhead

DONOR PROBLEMS

Maybe I will have a heart or kidney from a pig,
even at one hundred I will dance an Irish jig.
Could become an athlete when I hit five score and ten,
would I still be happy though? I couldn't say but then.
Will donor's psyche be considered in this brave new world?
Organs can remember! New fear that's just unfurled.

'Where's Grandad, Nana?' was the cry from little Baby Bunting,
'I think he's in the forest dear, it's time for truffle hunting.
It is a bit embarrassing but 'twas the life he chose,
The money comes in handy but it's ruining his nose.'

'I know I shouldn't tell you child he's cheating on the sly,
because he has two arms and legs he can climb into her sty.
Returning in the early hours in a most unsightly mess,
They say she is Vietnamese, an immigrant no less.'

'Anyway I mustn't carp, for gander so for goose,
your grandad ain't the only one playing fast and loose.
Tomorrow when he's visiting that bloated piece of ham.
I'll be in the meadow, with that cute li'le black-faced ram.'

'So my little lambkin with your farmyard go and play,
Take care of all the creatures, could be relatives one day.
I know that it's confusing and it sets your mind a whirl,
but just for now give thanks to God you're still a little girl.'

Derek B Hewertson

HAPPINESS

I have not reached the stars in all my days
Nor scaled the mountain tops
Or trod the vales.
I have not sailed the mighty Maine
Or walked through forest green
Or strayed upon a lonely plain.
I have not been in castles proud and strong
In palaces or mansions grand.
Or seen the sun rise in the East
Or set. Beyond this wondrous land.
And yet! I've heard a new-born baby cry
Held tiny hands and wiped an eye.
Held larger hands and guided footsteps frail
And all with joy and happiness that did not fail.
And in this smaller world of mine
The clouds may form or sun may shine.
'Tis then perchance I stand and dream
I'm such a small part of the planner's scheme.

D Adams

JIM

I once knew a fellow named Jim
Who ate raw onions on a whim.
He'd never had a cold
Or so I was told,
But who'd want to stand next to him!

B Eyre

DON'T PICK YOUR NOSE

Don't pick your nose
it makes me mad!
But I like it Mum
and it don't taste bad . . .
. . . and it's protein too,
and you know what they say,
you should have some protein every day!

Lynda J Smith

SAINT

There once was a horse called Saint
Who ran many races over hurdles with his mate
trying never to lose
he ended up with a bruise
that was almost the end of Saint
after seeing the birth of his foal called Kate

Kristina Howells

PHOBIC AEROBIC

Ursula Cunningham lives in Wick,
With a body as thin as a stick.
Until she became phobic
about her aerobics
and now she's as fat as a brick.
A gymnasium, she thought, was the trick
but the exercises made her feel sick.
It was so ironic
she wasn't bionic
because doing the splits was comic

Maureen Reynolds

GIFT

There was a time
when a man came down
from the mountain.
He joined our circle.
Our circle was a village,
turned into a town,
which became, in turn,
a city. This place
was our perception
of what we had been
told to expect.

This man didn't tell us
his name: we didn't ask it.
It seemed irrelevant,
as when he left
nothing had changed.

Those who expect a miracle
are surprised to discover
that the miracle is in the expectation.
As things that happen are as unimportant
- as things that we think may happen.

Uniqueness is the substance of our being.

On the day he left we felt the same.
he came and went as is the order of things.

The gift is love and life
- in life we lie no more alone
- through love we gain our freedom.

Being is the essence of our existence.

Michael Fenton

MAESTRO

One of the best things in my life
Has to be my car,
It's only an eleven year old banger,
But it's taken me quite far.
I bought it when I found that,
Walking hurt my knees,
If I had to give it up
I wouldn't be very pleased.
I use it for my shopping,
Or take my family out,
It costs me a bit to keep,
But it's worth it there's no doubt.
It gives me independence,
To go where I want to go,
You asked what's the best thing in my life?
And now you know.

F Baker

PURE LAUGHTER

One of the loveliest of sounds is innocent laughter,
The echo of joyfulness, bubbling enjoyment so carefree and young;
Silvery laughter like sunlight sparkling on water
Or bells being rung.

Not the snide, clever-dick sort of chortle, deep-rooted in malice
Delivered by warped, bitter humans, their laugh rightly named
'like a drain',
Not wasp-witted humour that sneers as the victim cringes,
Delighting in pain.

Ah, let us hear more of real laughter, uplifting and healing -
The full-throated guffaw, the peal of pure merriment, genuine mirth;
The radiance of friendship and joy that we hope for in Heaven
Foreshadowed on earth.

Christine Nicholls

MY SILVER REINDEER

Let's see the rainbow in your ring,
Then I'll tell you my loved best thing.
Child stroked the opal upon my hand,
Said, 'Do you believe in Faeryland?'
A story filled her little head 'Yes I do,
of course,' I said.
With solemn face she handed me the reindeer
off the Christmas tree
'He's silver and is terribly old,
as old as Mummy so I'm told.
I'm not allowed to play with him,
don't tell her that I've unhooked him,
Faeries are fond of pretty things,
and he's real silver match their wings.
One Christmas a goblin hid in the tree,
took him away when they had tea.
It was lucky he was found, for Faeryland is underground.
And have you ever been inside?'
'No but I have often tried.
Been with my spade out in the snow,
couldn't dig far enough below.
But every single snowman knows, for when
he melts it's where he goes.
Heaven is up, but Faeryland down,
seems funny she said with puzzled frown.
If men come back, they turn to dust,
my reindeer came without no rust.'
She paused and shook her curly head,
'Then how did he come back?' I said.
'A Saint Bernard dog which Mummy knows
found him deep down in the snows -
Return from Faeryland is rare,
guard your ring you must take care.

Girl faeries like to deck themselves
with pretty pearls and pink seashells.
Bright jewellery, love coloured slides,
They stole Aunt's cat with emerald eyes.
A china one with a cross face,
once sat inside her fireplace.
Elves in the holly wait at night
thieving, when switched off the light.
Christmas passed, all holly burn,
a berry left, they will return.
It's best behind the pictures feel,
seek every berry, stop them steal.
Aunt Emma's still has lost her cat,
never, will she get it back.
Mum says we'll have to wait and see,
they've broken it, it's plain to me.
You must never breathe a word,
his eyes are earrings so I've heard.
I love my reindeer best of all,
I'll stop the goblins ever call.
Not one berry will remain,
from us they'll never steal again!'

A E Doney

WAKING UP

Waking up next to you
The smell of your light brown hair.

The twinkle in your hazel eyes,
The smile that holds many a surprise.

The soft and gentle touch of you,
The way you run your fingers through your hair

The way you hold me,
A silent am here.

The awesome power of you, my lady M
Your slender legs
Your soft white skin
Your mischievous and perfect grin.

The scent of you
The awesome power in all of you.
It is true the best things in life are free
Like the love from you to me.

Jackie Stapleton

FAMILY

Best things in life come free
All my friends have to agree

There is no price for brother
There is nothing compared to mother

Share pain to friend or minister
Best performer is sister

All seasons are for love
No boundary, summer or Easter

Respect some, accept other
Door of heart open to father

Noor Shahzadi

LAMENT FOR THE TROLLEY-BUS

Oh, where have all the trolleys gone?
The trolley-buses once so seen
Across the land in times bygone,
Now passed from sight as never been,
But not from mind! In childhood days
In thirties age I can recall
Demise of trams and short-lived phase
Of trolley-bus, its rise and fall.

Tramcars' last day I stood beside
Illuminated tram whose path
Crowds followed in the hope of ride.
'Great service done!' its epitaph.

No more 'clang, clang' of bell; of wheels
No more the clatter, screech and squeals!

Freed from the tyranny of rails,
Though still restrained by wires o'erhead,
New-fangled trolley-bus prevails,
Resplendent in rich cream and red.
In summer hols at age of ten,
At start, alone, I'd jump aboard,
(No fear of molestation then!)
Top deck, front seat, the best on board!
Conductor rings; with scarce a sway,
With quick and smooth acceleration,
The trolley-bus gets under way . . .
For awe-struck youth, exhilaration!
Through Portsmouth town to Southsea's joys,
Via Hillsea, Copnor, 'neath blue skies,
The trolley glides, no smell, no noise . . .
It can take cyclists by surprise!

Arrived at South Parade Pier I make
For Punch and Judy, ice cream stall,
The pier's amusements, Canoe Lake,
All there a youngster to enthral!
Then all too soon time to return;
The trolley leaves with whirr and swish,
No fumes, no smell, no fuel to burn . . .
For smoother ride no one could wish.

Oh, why have all the trolleys gone?
Oh, why will planners never learn?
O, smelly, diesel beast - begone!
O, friendly trolley-bus - return!

Geoffrey Matthews

GARDENS

There are gardens that look a mess, others are a real pretty sight
They always look much better when the sun shines really bright
Cutting the grass making sure it has some feed
Making it look lush and getting rid of any weed
Insuring we have treated and mended the old fence
As against the north wind it's the garden's only defence

I turn the earth over, a worm pops up from the ground
If I dig really deep there's a lot more to be found
There's a buzzy bee just missing the top of my head
Thank goodness it's decided to settle in a rose instead
Here's a stream of ants marching in a straight line
They soon disappear in a crack which is very fine

So busy gardening I suddenly realise there's a smell
It's next door's barbecue, my nostrils begin to swell
Time to pack up now I really need a drink
Hands washed, wine poured, in the chair I sink
Hubby lights our barbecue, I can hear the sizzling of the
                                                    sausages and steak
In the kitchen I now go for the salad and rice to make

Sitting down to dinner we unwind with another glass of wine
The sun begins to go down but the weather is warm and fine
Looking around the garden it's lovely to see how everything has grown
I could spend many days like this just relaxing at home.

Kathy Prince

BEST THINGS

Each of these is dear to me.
Juicy grapes, refreshing tea,
Gigantic giant redwood tree,
Cauldronic chaos of the sea.

These give meaning to my life.
A planet free from war and strife.
Family love, outstanding treasure;
Time for thought and time for leisure.

The door for joy is open wide
If people care to peep inside.
Dispose of selfishness and greed.
Provide what others sorely need.

Recreate our wondrous Earth;
A new renaissance; joy of birth.
Priorities what real life means,
Fulfilling natural, mortal dreams.

They say the best in life is free;
A truth of pure simplicity.
The best in life is life itself
For him and her and you and me.

Ann Bryce

THE VISION OF HEAVEN

The Lord has given me a view of the other world,
Wings were given to me, and an angel attended me
From the city to a place that was bright and glorious,
The grass of that place was a living green and the birds
That were there warbled a sweet song,
The inhabitants were of all sizes, they were noble,
Majestic and lovely, they were the express image of Jesus
And their faces beamed, with holy joy,
Expressive of the freedom and happiness of the place,
The angel was singing and praising the holy lamb of God, holy, holy,
Come and walk through heaven's door.

I Lindo

FLORA

Flora dear Queen of Flowers
Is casting her magic spell
'rousing her sleeping beauties
In green fields and woodland dell.
First to waken, dear snowdrops
So dainty in white and green.
Shy little maids-in-waiting
To dear springtime's joyful scene.
Then she will gather sunbeams
And scatter them all around
Warming the earth so summer
Her great beauty can abound.
Weaving then a tapestry
In such colours to behold.
Shedding silver tears of joy
As each blossom does unfold.
Then when summer is over,
And long gone is autumn's glow.
Fragrant charges she will shield
From cruel winter's icy blow.

Violet M Corlett

A BEACH IN WINTER

A deserted beach in wintertime,
The wind blowing your hair.
The white tipped breakers pounding in,
The tang of salt in the air.

That bracing air of solitude,
Time to think, alone.
No one to distract you,
Nature on its own.

Wild sea, wild sky, primeval forces,
Man's battle with the elements.
Giant waves riding white horses,
An ever present challenge.

Dora Watkins

LOOK OUT

Look out at the world, is what I say
And if you see nought, but decay
Then there is something sadly wrong
Your faith in God is not so strong
But if the world is smiling through
There is so much hope for you.

Forget man and his latest trends
Look to where the rainbow blends
See jewels in the falling rain
Let not the blackbird sing in vain
Look out and there can be seen
A tree that is forever green
There's peace and beauty this we know
As we look out on the virgin snow
So look out and revel in what you see
The gathering clouds, a thrill can be.

Roland Seager

LET ME HAVE MY LIFE BACK PLEASE

The best things in life
Are waking up in morn
Think more of life than money
Given life when one is born
Some people say of this
Best things in life are free
So then who needs money
Just what will be, will be
In all of this confusion
My life it nearly stopped
And with a haunting echo
Out my grandfather plopped
Saying, please, please work hard
So bringing your life back
It maybe disbelieving
But almost on the right track.

M D Bedford

ODE TO A TIGRESS

I can see the look upon your face as you glance up to the skies
And the way you scan surrounding land with your amber coloured eyes
You've eaten of your dinner and you're lying fat and full
Resting and relaxing from your skirmish with the bull
It took a lot of energy for you to bring him down
But as his great head hit the floor you claimed your worthy crown
As evening nears you make a move. You're once more on the roam
Coming further that you wanted and a long way from your home
And pretty soon you'll have to find some place you can lie prone
Where you can have your little ones then you won't be alone
And after you have had your young the fun begins again
For you will have to kill then bring the food that you have slain
The circle of life will carry on no matter what you do
And I will have enjoyment as I keep on watching you.

V Barrasin

ONE MAN'S INSPIRATION
(For BG)

In forest mists
In autumn,
Amidst moist leaves
Of Fall,
Grows secretly
And silently
Caps of leather
Soft.
There are scarlet
Bright
And yellow hues,
Creams
And mushroom browns.
Shell-like forms
On bark of trees.
Orange dust specks
Blackened twigs.
But just on
Very special days
As nature's always true,
Silver threads
Of fairy's yarn
Are spun
To catch
The
Dew!

Lyn Sandford

LITTLE THINGS

Tiny seeds of happiness
           are only little things
falling feathers
           gossamer of fairy wings
sun's little fingers
           touching our earth
first rosebud
           bursting into birth
Venus, first star
           trembling into gold
a secret snowdrop
           sentinel in the cold
clouded shadows
           running over land
a touch of rain
           falling on my hand
warmth of a cat
           curled up in a chair
a soft gentle kiss
           on my cheek, just here.

T M Webster

MY FAVOURITE SIGHT

Oh to be enveloped by countryside!
Trees invite me with arms open wide!
Beckoning eagerly with green waving fronds.
To free me from suburban bonds!

Emerald castles stretch up to the sky.
A protective shield for passers-by!
Splashed with black shadow from overhead cloud!
Windswept pines so gracefully bowed.

Contoured scenery around me unfold.
Its magnet drawing into its hold!
Spellbound by mountains, majestic and strong!
Hypnotic power pulls me along!

Grass-covered slopes cascade into the lake.
Craving its cool refreshment to take.
Icy cold waters calling out my name.
'Bathe in me, then you'll be glad you came!'

Frothing foam shaping the weathered rocks, on its way.
Pure white waters rush to meet the bay!
Straying droplets splashing across my face,
Invite me into their fond embrace!

Weeping willows bathe branches in swirling streams!
Telling sad tales, revealing their dreams!
Offering me shade on a hot summer's day.
'Cool yourself, you know you can stay!'

Sun-captured daffodils, snowdrops so white!
This is part of my favourite sight.
Peace and tranquillity, absence of strife!
These have to be the best things in life!

Val Spall

THE PEARL OF FLOWERS

My petals are pink edged white
I have a golden sun in the middle,
I close when evening comes
Can you solve the riddle?

My name comes from the Anglo Saxon
Translated it means 'day's eye',
Also known as the 'pearl of flowers'
In times that have passed by.

My name was connected to a French royal
Marguerite de Valois was her name,
Whose jewels were a necklace of pearls
Linked up to form a chain.

So on hot balmy summer days
As little girls play on the grass,
They have been known to pick me
And create one, as time to pass.

And after much deep concentration
I turn out to be anything but just plain,
They delicately place me round their necks
Yes, I am the daisy, that makes the chain.

Margaret M Donnelly

MY WEDDING GOWN

Dazzling in the sunlight
Like crystal stalactites
Prisms flashing colours
Blinding to the sight.

Shimmering in sunshine
Resplendent in my view
The gown I wore so proudly
The day I married you

Bittersweet are memories
Of a day so far away
Yet still I keep my wedding gown
Safely packed away

Its beauty hasn't faded
It's there for all to see
But the girl has gone who wore it
Now I see only me.

Linda Cooper

IS THIS ART?

Have you seen the sunrise of a brand new dawn
A flower's petals - or a field of corn -
The lines in the grass of a new mown lawn.
Seen the cobweb with jewels of dew,
A woodland with bluebells - oh so blue
Azaleas of every hue -
Is this art?

Have you seen the colours in a butterfly's wing,
Or listened to a blackbird sing.
Looked at the beauty of a magpie's wing,
The fresh green colours as leaves unfold
The wonder of autumn - bronze and gold,
The lines in the face of someone old -
Is this art?

Millions of stars in a velvet sky,
A long tailed comet flying by -
A crescent moon to catch your eye
Is this art?

The changing canvas is my eye
And all is framed within.
The artist - Mother Nature
Just in case you're wonderin'.

Janet Fludder

ALIVE

Petite. Genteel Stalks.
Protuberant leaves. Growing in shade.

As a child, I picked primroses for my parents.
Mam put them in a little glass vase tinted green
and shaped like a tulip. The vase made it look
as though the primrose was still growing in a wood.

Barry Welburn

JOY

Whether I live in a mansion
Or in one very small room;
I must have my special things . . .
Fine bone china and objects d'art;
Books and pictures on the walls,
Growing plants and some flowers . . .
Whether in town or country
There must be a view . . .
Trees and fine buildings
To inspire one anew.
I must have music,
Stimulating . . . relaxing
To nurture one's soul
And bring peace of mind . . .
These are God's greatest gifts . . .
The ability to see and feel.

Helen Persse

NINE TO FIVE

Nine to five, no more
As a pensioner I have scored
Dreaming of laying in bed until nine
A marvellous thought in wintertime
However, this won't happen
Grandchildren will be the pattern
Keeping us on our feet
Paying out for treats,
Am I selfish to wish
For no more nine to five-ish?

Nine to five no more
How would my time score,
Rise at nine
The world is mine
No need to wear a watch
Time has stopped
There I go, dreaming dreams
Of what should have been
While children scheme
My every scene.

Barbara R Lockwood

BEST THINGS IN LIFE

My portrait gallery is by far
The thing in life I treasure most;
A century and a half of memories
Collected - and not lost.

Faces of long ago
Stances and poses set,
Expressions hard to fathom
Body language to interpret.

He looks grave, she looks kind,
A dominant and submissive one?
Mutual tenderness and caring
It's hard to say - now they are gone.

They span a century of change
Neither one could read or write,
Signed their names with a cross
Exchanging vows their troth to plight.

What would they make of today's world?
The space age, global travel
The marvels of modern medicine
The internet to unravel.

Today we think we're in control
Pushing through frontiers, juggling permutations,
Focusing through the microscope
Genetic engineering, organ transplantations.

Their lives were short and very hard
But trustful of the will of God,
Content with their lot they seemed to say
'Thy will be done' in each and every day.

Beryl Moorehead

THE DAY YOU LEFT ME

Darkness fetched such sadness that cold night in November
Your little body shook then you passed away.
The joy and love you had given me over the years now gone forever
Still the memories of my loyal companion will remain within my heart
The tears streamed down my face, your tiny grave had to be dug
Wrapped in a soft blanket I gently laid you on the earth
Under the tree by the wall where you used to sit.
The thought that your sweet face would not look up at me again
was almost too much to bare
I gently put the wet soil back in place covering the hole
'Titch' a simple cross now marks your grave
Forget-me-nots have been planted to flower each spring
A simple tribute to you, my friend, you were one of the best
things in my life
The time may come in the near future when another
Jack Russell puppy may come to live with me
The clouds of darkness will lift and I'll smile again when I
think of you.

Pamela M Wild

PARAGONS OF PLEASURE

I've lived with moles in a wood,
Accompanied knights to seek the grail.
Ridden on a unicorn
Travelled hill and dale.

Middle earth, Fionavar,
I've visited various worlds.
In imagination, all is possible,
Each volume is a pearl.

Each page I turn, each book I read
Each character I meet
Allows me to accompany them
On journeys and great feats.

Heroes, every one of them
To me, they always seem.
Read and revisited often,
They allow me many dreams.

By sea or flight, in ancient times,
Wherever they must go,
To find what it is they're looking for
Page turns before I know.

And so with mixed emotion
Each friend is stored away,
Upon a bulging bookcase
Saved for another day!

Tree

THE SGWD YR ELRA WATERFALL WALK

As we started our walk on a crisp winter's day
The sun shone so brightly and lit up the way.
Through trees so tall and paths that were steep,
We walked and we talked as we shuffled our feet.

The birds in the river were looking for fish
As they hopped and they sang with a very high pitch.
The sounds were so wonderful, the air was so fresh
And the best was to come, as we stopped for a rest.

We walked through the woods, as still as could be,
When a wondrous sound we could hear with glee.
Water cascading, the spray was so fresh,
We moved even closer, it was the best feeling yet.

Our skins felt like velvet, our clothes were all wet,
But a shower in a waterfall, what could we expect.
As the water came faster we smiled with delight,
Nowhere else had we seen a more glorious sight.

Christine Licence

THE BEACH AT SOUTHWOLD

A row of neat and slatted wooden huts
Small coloured icons of a bygone grander age,
Proudly polished, painted, named
All monuments in miniature,
Wind breaks, shelters from the elements,
Our private little look-out posts
We sit snug, a warm, safe, huddled group,
Kerosene-lit faces half shadowed in the dusk.

Today we watched the canvas of your lives
Distant fishermen in gale tossed boat,
Tall man, small boy, collecting shells or kicking sand,
Soft thudding footfalls sprinting by,
Then rolled up trouser legs to paddle
Ankle deep in icy water.
And cosy matrons, plump and sunk in deckchairs,
Dozing, reading, sewing, knitting,
Dreaming of those other days.
We saw old men, spread-eagled on the sand,
Bellies rising, falling with the tide.

We heard the young girls' laughter
Fresh faces keen and turned towards the sky,
Blowing hair and rising, flapping skirts
To tease and tantalise young men, in long-limbed groups,
Striding out and running free,
Shirts full in the wind, white billowing sails
Riding the high seas, breasting the waves of youth,
Exhilarated and intoxicated with the wind,
The wild, wide spaces only seen in dreams.

Carmel Wright

PRIDE OF PLACE

It's just a pretty picture too
Hanging on the kitchen wall.
Tied tight with ribbons of blue.
It's painted with a garden small
Full of red and yellow flowers
And a white cottage with windows neat.
Light reflects in daytime hours
Upon pink roses rambling sweet.
But if the words that mean a lot
For it's like a little prayer
Giving thanks for what you got,
Making it beyond compare.
Here in my little kitchen like a bee so busy
Often I stop and pause awhile.
As these lines come back to me,
It still makes me smile
Recalling so many a happy time.
Delicious smells of home baking crisp and brown.
Summing up my favourite rhyme.
Oh what a joy I found
All the simple pleasure it brought.
In each lovely word
Always plays a part.
Of the most beautiful verse I ever heard.
Which now I can recite off by heart.
Cheery as the kettle singing its song.
Helps me though my task each day.
But often my thoughts wonder upon.
These words Lord bless my home I pray.

M Hanmer

THE GREAT OUTDOORS

Swimming, in a warm sea,
Is part of summer for me,
Nowhere, I would rather be,
Floating there, on my back,
Mind and body, going slack,
Looking up the sky,
Hearing seagulls, when they cry,
Cradled by cliff and sand,
Enjoying a picnic, or local band,
The clock strikes, I realise,
Heading back, would be wise,
And I walk along the seashore,
A summer day, ended once more,
Everything, quiet as a mouse,
Walking back to the guest house,
The evening meal, over I fear,
Still warm, though evening's here,
A time to enjoy, 'the great outdoors',
Summertime on beach, or moors,
The moorland air, and sandy floors.

Sheila Walters

BEST THINGS IN LIFE

Many a time you hear people say: 'Best things in life are free'
Oh how unsound, here's what I've found
Nothing splendid and worthy comes easy

Undeterred by, sometimes, friction, misunderstanding, or contrarieties,
Exchanging pride and singularity for compromise and love
Family and friends who matter
In times of need,
Stand shoulder to shoulder.

Pain to bring forth, pain while upbringing
Notwithstanding, many sleepless nights
Being found worthy of such a precious gift
Someone to love and cherish and call your own
Yes! Children are the crest of the best things in life
Which comes with a price and great sacrifice.

No creditors knocking at your door
Having enough money for basic necessity
And a sunshine holiday occasionally
A job to enjoy and a home full of toys
Are among life's best things for me.

Peace and joy experienced in the midst of conflict and sadness
Patience exercised during trials and testing
Gentleness and goodness employed in the bosom of authority
Meekness applied in the heart of great fame
Open-mindedness and faith
All made possible only through love
Form the crown of the best things in life.
So you see?

Joyce Peter

ME AND YOU AND A DOG NAMED BOO

Hold my hand as we watch her crashing through the undergrowth.
A flurry of fur, lost ball, failing duck's wings and leaves.
She emerges, frustrated again by the untimely end to her chase
as the duck soars into the air, squawking its indignance.
We smile at her amusing antics and steal a kiss in the rain -
or the snow or the sunshine.
Again she appears, black and white head cocked to one side,
anxious at our disappearance.
We retrieve the lost ball and return it to the safety of her muddy mouth.
No doubt to be lost once more when something more interesting
becomes available.
She smiles as only she can, her eyes - one brown and one blue - so full
of expression and joy, as she careers down the muddied riverbank.
Her wintry white legs now black with dirt.
Her snout blackened with enjoyment.
My trousers always muddy at the back, your top splattered with
mud from your usual futile attempts to run and hide from her.
In the wind, the rain, the snow, the scorching heat - it doesn't matter.
For these are the best of times.
Me and you and a dog named Boo.

Rachael Poyle

Summer In Portugal

In your deep blue hue the seagulls fly
While the windmill sails turn slowly round
While the patient sea waits for the nets to dry
Large stone wheels ensure the grain is ground

Your golden sand washes smooth and clean
While the sun's fingers tease open the cloud
Aged and worn timbers glisten in the sheen
As the seagulls fly and scream aloud

Majestic rock etched away by the sea
Still breaking away by the ebb and flow
Away on the horizon an island calls to me
Before the scent of night says it's time to go

As my summer in Portugal begins to fade
The sails on the mill still turn in the shade.

Colin Skilton

MY PETS

I love my two
  Four legged pets.
They mean the world to me.
  Living alone in my country home
They keep me company
  Perhaps I should explain.
    They are not the same.
One has wool
  And one has fur,
My cat is a him
  My sheep is a her.
The cat lives in
  The sheep lives out.
But both obey me
  When I shout.

Irene Millington

HILLSIDE THOUGHTS

The distinct colours of the immediate landscape
glide swiftly beyond reach
to merge gently with distant blue,
a strange compassionate silence grips me,
soothes my mind,
protects me from the advancing threat
of a melting world -
greed, corruption, ridicule,
a solitary hawk,
unfettered by circumstance,
soars majestically . . .
the air is windless
and life is peaceful;
here among the undulating hills
I have found my 'Shangri-la'.

Arthur Pickles

I BELIEVE IN LOVE

This made me think hard and strong
In this world where we belong
Thinking about the hate, cruelty and war
It was from a different angle that I saw
It's not the best things we've got
But what are we missing such a lot
What this world needs now is love, sweet love
Love one's neighbour as one's self
Leave no one sitting on the shelf
Forget the racial and religious fights
Keep love always in your sights
Help each other in many ways
You'll find that you have happier days
Let us stop these wars and greed
By helping others in great need
Don't let possessions mean more than a friend
For he'll stand by you until the end
So please I beg you think of love
As the best thing in your life

Flora Passant

THE SWALLOWS OF PORTUGAL

The world is very beautiful,
Our God created *all,*
He made everything so perfect,
From the smallest to the tall.

I love the flowers and animals,
The apples in the Fall,
But nothing is more magical,
As the swallows in Portugal.

Among the cliffs and rocky heights,
They dart and climb on wing,
I watched their flight by day and night,
And listened to them sing.

I take the plane and go by train,
Cross miles and miles of sea,
How can they so small and fay,
Travel as far as me?

Back home again, there's wind and rain,
And I long for a spring-like day,
What do I see bringing joy and glee,
But the swallows, they've followed me!

Margaret Findlay

DRAGON ON AN ORANGE WALL

In the dining room upon an orange wall
Hangs a picture in a wide and wooden frame
Of a dragon breathing fire and flame,
And on the dresser top for all to view
Is a painting by Joshua, aged two.
Dark brown blobs and lines and yellow splashes,
Painted with his Jackson Pollock brushes.
The other day in the golf store,
He raised a golf club in the air,
Good strong grip and stance and sway,
His grandfather was heard to say.
'Another Tiger Woods is on his way.'
Now he's back home in his dining room
With the dragon on the orange wall,
Sitting in his own high chair -
'Put on his bib - don't let him dribble,
Give him paper, pad and let him scribble.'
What's he drawing? We're not sure,
But it's looking like a Henry Moore.

Stewart Gordon

JOURNEYING

Undecided, on the great road, a dog trotting ahead
Windy, on that road, and a moon rising
A wagon passes, then Securicor, and the salt marshes
With the mountains ahead, we are rich
With the music on the wind, the mountains seem to approach.

Michael Soper

LADY

Lady is my Doberman, but there's collie in her too,
She can always make me laugh out loud,
When sometime I feel blue.
Asleep on her back with her paws in the air,
Forget the TV, I just have to stare,
At the waving and twitching sight before me,
With accompanying whines, such a thing to see.

Ears a-twitching and teeth on show,
Whole body rippling and tail on the go.
Eyebrows dancing up and down,
I laugh aloud at my big, black clown.
Then she wakes and stares at me,
She gives her smile while still sleepy.
She'll stretch with her bottom in the air,
Often windy sounds emit from there.

Strolling over, she sits, with her paw on my knee,
Grinning I take it, as it's offered to me.
The doggy smile is still on her face,
As she ambles back to her comfy place.
Soon she's sleeping, down for the night,
I feel content, everything is now right.

Ann Simpson

MY FURRY FRIEND

He came into the garden to climb his favourite tree,
The funny antics he produced did fill me with glee.
Just a little kitten but was he having fun,
Through the plants and flowers how he could run.

He got more friendly and in the house he came,
This loveable ball of fluff, Sandy was his name.
For food he could not often wait,
He would try to help himself putting in the tin his paw,
Then licking it all across his jaw.

As we were lying in our bed getting off to sleep,
Under the bedclothes so quietly he would creep.
Silence was broken, as loudly he would purr,
You just couldn't help loving that bundle of fur.

Evelyn M Harding

MY FAVOURITE THINGS

Whenever I think of my favourite things
Thinking of the joyous sounds, in spring
The thrush who sings, his songs of praise
A flute-like whistle repeated at each phrase

The harsh noisy rattle of the blackbird's song
Hunting for insects, and spiders, as he hops along
For his offspring, as his mate guards them with care
Away from the enemy's clutch, or the magpie's glare

Such confident, tame birds, so full of cheer
As the thrush listens, and sits on a twig, quite near
He joins the blackbird, till they soar through the sky
Uttering different notes, while they still hunt, and fly

Such blessings are seen, as the love birds steal a kiss
Through the joyous of spring she blushes, but, oh what bliss
She peeps this way and that way, thinking 'Oh what fun
As the mist is swept away, with the miracles of the sun

While the daffodils spring out, showing their yellow faces
And the primroses blooms, with fragrance and graces
Such a picturesque scene, throughout these shining hours
Through God's powerful Hand, and the help of light showers

Till, the shadows fail, and the sun goes down
The birds fly back to their nest, one by one
The showers cease, when the twilight appears
The flowers seem to sleep, as the sun disappears

All is at rest, through the cool of the night
The birds nestle together, underneath the pale moonlight
These words I express, are my favourite things
The best things that are free, through God's blessings in the spring

Jean P Edwards McGovern

Our Mum

She worked so hard all her days, without complaint only smiles,
Wiping runny noses, mopping fevered brows, kissing hurt away,
She loved us and protected us each step along life's rocky way,
Watched us take our first faltering steps, my sister, brother and me,
We gave her grief when we were bad, it wasn't meant, she'd
                                   understand,
Always there with a helping hand, we never went without,
Gave us values, made us strong, was proud of us, we could do
                                   no wrong,
She had her pain, but hid it well, and no one saw the tears that fell,

We all grew up, went separate ways, made families of our own,
Happy and contented she was to see all her children grown,
As years rolled by and to our shame, to us she always was the same,
We never saw the slowing pace, tired eyes, the breathless sighs,
It's our turn now to pamper her, to show how much we care,
And to let her know that in our hearts, she will always be there,
A mother's love is more precious than gold, love that can never be
                                   bought or sold,
We thank you for all you've done to us, you are the world's best . . .
                                   our mum.

Helen Posgate

WILLOW

The silken kiss of silver catkins,
The sweet perfume of summer flowers,
The burnished leaves of autumn,
The graceful swish of the wind blown willow.

The silken touch of your lips,
Your sweet perfume you bring to me,
The highlights in your hair,
The way you move that's oh so fair.

These are the things I see in thee,
Condemn me not, tho I liken you to a tree.

J W Murison

THE BALL

Smart men in kilts hold champagne glasses,
Black, among the floral wash of colour.
Each woman adorned by petalled gown,
Spreading skirts enhance each graceful stem.

Each specimen has developed differently,
Unique, cultivated by gardeners,
Paid for their expertise in flower heads,
Carefully watered and trimmed.

The hall is filled with tinkling laughter,
A delightful array of moving colour,
As a show, each bloom examined by florist
Who know and choose their preference, though

The flowers may not just be picked,
Rarely guarded and gently enticed.
Some flowers start to wither in the heat,
The kilts will see them home.

And as the evening dusk approaches,
Flowers close, prepare for morning,
In the dimming light, they dance
Away, to their place beneath the soil.

Jillian Shields

CHILDREN'S INNOCENCE

Jessica age four
Got the scissors again . . .
Cut her fair hair then
Brother Morgan's age one.

Dad rescued the situation
With a bit of titivation . . .
A good trim to both their heads,
Then sent them off to their beds.

Mum said, 'Our little Jessica
Had played at cutting hair at school
Not in the school rule . . .
Jessica learnt a good thing to
Not to stick their fair hair back with glue.'

Mum's tum is getting bigger . . .
Jessica listens to baby's heartbeat
Her innocence complete . . .
Tries to draw a scribble figure.

Lord please help my family to survive
Post angels to shield their fearless eyes
From influences that cause them harm . . .
Fill their lives with laughter and surprise
And Lord please keep us all calm.

Lesley J Worrall

THE UNICORN

It stands so proud on a windy hill,
This unicorn is very still,
Is it in my dreams that this creature exists?
Waiting eternally for the maiden's kiss.

This elusive soul from another time,
Has a golden horn and mane so fine,
An untamed spirit belonging to no one,
The untouchable myth is free to run.

Is it in my mind that the unicorn lives,
Unique and powerful the feeling it gives?
Myths and legends surround its being,
Strong and proud is the beauty you're seeing!

To exist forever in someone's dreams,
To live in the realms of kings and queens,
This mysterious creature, oh so rare,
Will be forever, if you dare!

Pamela Dickson

YOU MAKE US SO PROUD . . .

From the moment you were born
We've held you so tenderly, so close;
From all life's pleasures there givest,
We've always loved you, you've been the best

As you've grown, wonder and beauty embalmed,
Our sweetest li'l girl, always, on our mind;
Our baby; our daughter; our beautiful child,
We love you our sweet Lynsey, more than our own lives

The formative years may have seen some struggles,
As you found out wrong from right;
But the times you felt we didn't love you so,
caused us pain and darkened the longest night . . .

But you're our child, borne of love and we do love you so;
We will love you always, forever you will be, our baby;
And we're watching you still, as you've grown into a beautiful woman,
You make us so proud to be, your mummy, your daddy,
You are our Lynsey, you are our whole life,
you are undoubtedly, the best thing, in our life . . .

Ron Matthews Jr

SNOOPY MY CAT

This is a story about my cat
He is black and white and fairly fat.
He is friendly, good-natured and will never miss
To lift up his head and give me a kiss.
He has very long hair which is smooth and clean
Except when he wanders into the shrubs so green.
At night he likes his beauty care
He sits by the mirror and I comb out his hair,
And while he's been tended
He purrs his best,
Then lies down and has his rest.
He loves to be, wherever I am,
Sits on my desk as quiet as a lamb.
Tries to take the pen from my hand
And flicks it on the floor where I stand.
He crosses the road to see his friend Mitt
But I get so worried in case he gets hit.
He makes me happy when I am sad
And is always there when I am glad.
It is a joy to see him play,
And I'm sure he knows what I say.
His name is Snoopy,
And if you're not aware
His paw shoots out and gives you a scare.

Margaret Kelly

MEDITATION ON THE SUN

As I watched the sun go down
Beyond the glistening sea,
The glory of its reflected light
Reached across me,
Filling my heart with gratitude
And a sense of security
That life upon this beautiful Earth
Would never cease to be
Nurtured by this mighty source
Of love's infinite energy;
Thus thought I, midst all those things
That demand of us a fee,
The sun alone remained the best
Thing in life that is *free!*

C Warren-Gash

THE LANE

The lane swirled
by the tide of night
becomes the harbour
of all my thoughts,
despairs
and hopes.
The lane
sanded by tree banks
and sea dark;
becomes a place
to gently drift at times
to where, high at its source,
I see a moon
through trees of lace
and honeycomb
and wonder;
as in a gentle breeze
a change of silent leaves
clutch at its misty light,
and at my mind.

John Wiltshire

WARMING DAYS

Of the best things in life
that of country walks, that of a warming day,
those trees so bold, of those country lanes, as we walk or stroll,
on our way, this of a warming day.
Those trees so bold
and birds of song, country lanes, sky of blue light,
summer clouds soon to clear, a sky of blue, field of green,
birds of song, as we walk that of country lanes.

Those canals and lakes that we see,
of swans, that glide along with ease and ducks that swim
up and down with that of water, with reach of green.
This of the best things for, to see as we walk,
that of country lanes, with trees so bold, birds of song
and warming days of summer time.
Watch lilies that float.

Canals, lakes, swans, ducks with chicks,
trees so bold, lanes we walk of summer days, sky of blue, birds of song,
favourite things life as we walk those country lanes, and pubs to seek,
on our travels, while we walk and make our way.
These of the best things in life, to what we have in times so bad.
Canals, lakes, swans that glide with grace.
Ducks that swim with chicks following behind.
Mountain streams and flowing brooks.
Lanes we walk, trees so bold, sky of blue.
Lanes we walk, in times so bad, those birds of song,
field of green, mountains, hills, sky of blue,
pubs we find of country ways.

A May

FREE TIME

The time when I can relax,
sit back and be myself for a while.
No need to worry who is watching me,
time to think, to plan, to smile.
Time to spend with my family,
to listen to music, or to write.
Free time begins on Friday,
and ends on Sunday night.
It consists of annual leave,
bank holidays and weekends.
Days that are very special to me,
days when I am with friends.
These days are my reward for working,
for fulfilling a father's role.
A task I carry out willingly,
always staying in control.
Time that passes so quickly,
and soon becomes part of history.
Free time that is so important,
and means so much to me.

M A Challis

BRIDGES

Life's bridges that we all must cross,
secure within our mother's womb,
to sudden shock of light imposed.
This bridge is eased by arm's embrace,
and flow of suckled nipple's milk.

Love and protection always there,
while growth makes us more curious.
Till only warning words are left,
as youth enforces its own will.

Then bridge of puberty is met,
with signs that we are self-assured.
But we don't know what's not divulged.
The complex sway of rope made bridge.

Choices arrive, decisions made,
of where we think our talents lie.
So we strive to cross the bridge of
learning, to unfurl ambitions.

But all is futile if not shared
with mate, with who we true relate.
So now is sought the strength of steel,
to bridge two personalities.

Fullness of good, life has to hold,
is to be found in union bound.
With children borne, experience shared,
complete cycle's continuance.

Fast sped our years, now fully spent,
we've time to ponder our success.
Breeched obstacles, both fair and foul,
but left is void of what will lie
across life's final bridge we'll take.

Leslie Fine

BEST THINGS IN LIFE ARE FREE

Best things in life are free,
We don't need to plead on bended knee.
To run or dance, to skip or walk,
To laugh or cry, to shout or talk.
To hear or see, to smell or touch,
A smile can mean so very much.
Love, loyalty, trust and hope,
Gives one strength and courage
and the will to cope.

Best things in life are free,
I wonder with me do you agree?
A words of advice spoken sincerely,
A word of comfort needed dearly.
A word of hope and encouragement,
A wonder of tender endearment,
Gives one's life a purpose and meaning,
When friends show love and understanding
with true and honest feeling.

Best things in life are free,
Nature in all its glory inspires me.
Birds great and small are my delight,
Sweet scented snowdrop clad in pure white.
Butterflies and dragon flies mesmerise me so,
Streams and brooks tinkle and tides ebb and flow.
Trees I admire, silhouetting the sky, proud and tall,
The farm animals, I love them all.
My many dogs and cats I happily recall, I miss them all.

The best things in life are free,
I don't need to plead on bended knee
for the love of my husband and family.
I have never known a time without my sisters,
they are so very dear to me.

E M Crellin

GUESS WHO?

Who is that fellow over there
Sitting upright on the chair?
Around his neck a bow is tied
And he looks so glassy eyed.

There's nothing else I'd rather be
A teddy's life is not for me
And as for dark ships in the night
Well, I would rather fly a kite.

For I would rather be myself
Although he's landed on the shelf
My life's companion over there
Why of course it's Edward Bear!

Norma Macarthur

THE CARDBOARD KISSES

If by bad chance I had a fire and one thing I could rescue,
I'd rush to grab an envelope that contains a card from you.
The closest treasure to my heart is a simple Christmas card,
containing cardboard kisses that you pressed down very hard.
For you barely saw what you were writing on that oh so fateful day,
for the next you lapsed in coma 'til our Lord took you away.
The final card you wrote me that said you loved me so,
we'd no idea the end was near, so close your time to go.
Beloved mum, I treasure every single word you wrote,
enclosed within that envelope your last, your final note.
What other treasure could I want? What else could I hold so dear
than that final words you wrote to me to keep you to me near?
A simple card, a robin, sitting singing in a tree
means more than all the gold on earth as it was written just for me.
The shaky writing hard to read, containing loving wishes,
but best of all the final line that abounds with cardboard kisses.

Channon Cornwallis

A Cuppa

A cup of tea the English say
Sit down, feet up, you'll have to stay
It's half-past, the eleven
That's way past a brew
Come on, sit down, we'll have no more ado

A cup of tea the English say
It wouldn't seem right, an odd sort of day
If passing by the half of the hour
It would be most unthinkable
Like warm milk, undrinkable

A cup of tea the English say
In bone china cups, it's the only way
Three bags, to the pot, and poss it well
Milk in first, then slowly fill
For the taste, like friendship
We don't want to kill.

Michael Widdop